DESTINED
FOR MORE

A Broken Girl's Journey of Chasing Dreams and Killing Giants

BRANDY BELL

This book is dedicated to the broken, to the weary, and to the wounded. It is dedicated to every single one of you who has been told no, or that you are not good enough. It is dedicated to those who have been doubted and disregarded. Let's go on this journey together and find out exactly what we are made of.

And to my eighteen-year-old self. You are going to make so so many mistakes along the way. Huge ones. Be brave and give yourself grace. It's gonna be ok. Just don't ever become famous. Too much dirt.

TABLE OF CONTENTS

INTRODUCTION

"Everything is impossible until it's done."
—Nelson Mandela

The thought of telling my personal story is terrifying to say the least. I mean, who really wants the world to know what's hiding in their junk drawers? And yes, I get that everyone has skeletons—mine just seem to be dressed crazier than others. (And surely, they were drinking when they put those outfits on.) However, I keep coming back to the idea that if I can share my story, then, just maybe, I can help convince at least one other person to fearlessly pursue whatever they were designed, called, and gifted to be. I hope that holds true for you. Because you are capable of chasing down your dreams. Regardless of where you are, where you have been, or how many littles you have at home.

Together we will make our way through the somewhat tattered, occasionally torn, often sad, and yet somehow comical pages of my story. Including the parts I have spent 45 years NOT talking about. So why I am I opening up now? Well…the short answer is this: I have spent the last 15 years teaching and encouraging woman like you to overcome obstacles, to chase down dreams, and to do the hard stuff it will take to live your best life. The one you were created for. And I want you to know that I have been in the trenches right there with you. Broken. Battered. Ready to give up.

From the outside, my life looks pretty idyllic. Especially since the invention of social media. I have a kind, handsome, loving husband who dotes on me and whom I adore. But what you don't see is before that amazing husband, I had to recover from years of abuse and fear. I have been blessed with a very long and successful career that many people would love to have. But what you don't see is the doors that were slammed in my face, and the "no's" that came more frequently than my Amazon deliveries. I have beautiful college-educated children, who are also chasing their dreams. But before those children graduated college, we had to overcome learning disabilities, racial ignorance, poverty, and all the challenges that came with teenage pregnancy and single parenting. The home we live in now (The Little Teeny Farm) is my dream home and I've been lucky enough to have it photographed for books and media. But before this beautiful home came along, me and three small boys stayed in a variety of unsavory places, included a motel and a tiny trailer that smelled like feet. There are lots of not-so-pretty parts that have led to where I am now. A botched surgery. The degenerative disease in my tailbone. My mother's mental illness. My father's death. My brother's death. My sister's death. You get the idea.

I want to share these things now, so you understand that you, too, have what it takes. You do. It's easy for us to find reasons why we cannot or should not do something. Legit reasons. What I'm hoping to do is to help you see that those reasons do not need to stop you. None of them are strong enough to hold you back from what you were created to do. When you're done reading this, my prayer is that you have a strengthened belief in yourself and that it sparks a wildfire of goal crushing and dream chasing. So, I am going to share with you my dirty laundry. My ginormous messes. My gnarled roots. My hurdles. My screw ups. My mountains. My giants. My failures AND my wins. Because behind all the successes in my life is just a broken girl who didn't give up. A broken girl who knew, somehow, she was destined for more.

When you close this book, I hope you have laughed and cried and stomped your foot and decided that you are not going to let anything get in your way. Because you have been called to do something that no one else has. You, too, are destined for more. And it's time that you get started.

Love,

Brandy Bell

CHAPTER 1

FAIRY TALES AND MISMATCHED SHOES

Leave the Past in the Past

> *"Find our who you are and do it on purpose."*
> —*Dolly Parton, Tweet, April 18, 2015*

As a little girl, I was half tomboy and half girly girl. I was scrawny, scrappy, and had a head of wild blonde curls that were prone to getting knotted to the point of dreads. They were as defiant as I was. I was equal parts salty and sweet, and as likely to whack you as I was to hug you. My hobbies included decorating dollhouses and climbing trees. I loved pretty dresses and mud. But I didn't mix the two. That's an accurate description of me to this day.

When I was in first grade, I remember a teacher pulling me out of class to speak to me. She had long, flowing locks of strawberry blonde hair and she smelled of roses and soap. I liked it. The day she pulled me into the hall, I remember her using a soft, kind voice. She was trying to encourage me to brush my hair and wear more appropriate clothes to school. (And if that was one of the many days that I dressed myself, who knows what I was wearing?) I remember her kneeling down, looking me in the eyes, and telling me that I would look so pretty if I brushed my hair. I didn't really understand it at the time, but looking back, I think she was just trying to help me. Help me not get picked on. Help me fit in. Help me not have reasons to fight all the other children. I think she knew my mama wasn't always able to do so.

I grew up with a workaholic dad and a mom who suffered from lots of mental issues. She could be very sweet and loving but many days operated on the level of an adolescent. Her moods determined how she parented. Brushing my hair and bathing were often optional. And you never knew how I would show up to school. Possibly in a wrinkly Sunday dress with mismatched shoes, topped off with a muddy cowboy hat that failed to tame my hair. Those were the days my mother encouraged me to express myself because she didn't have the energy to get out of bed. However, the next day could look totally different. If she was feeling energetic and parental, I may be sporting a perfectly coiffed ballerina bun, seersucker dress, and white leather sandals. It was impossible to predict. Even as a little teeny girl I was confused. (Squirrel: To this day I have no particular style. I may wear a flowy boho dress one day with messy side braids, and the next day a preppy tailored short set complete with…wait for it…a neckerchief. I love neckerchiefs.) The only reason I was not a complete train wreck in my elementary years was because I was blessed with an amazingly "proper" grandmother who quickly stepped in to fill some gaps. Thank goodness, because who wants to be the stinky kid?

Even with all her issues, there were many wonderful things I learned from my mama. She was kind and absolutely nonjudgmental. She loved ALL people. Everybody, always. She was like Bob Goff, but unstable. She was super encouraging. And absolutely believed I could do anything. She not only pushed me as an artist—she made sure I always had art supplies on hand, even if that meant wrapping her own canvases for me to paint on. Because she was crafty, and I was hard on things, she was also regularly fixing things for me. Like the rhinoceros' horn on one of my paper dolls, after I "accidentally" ripped it off when he was misbehaving.

She was a great decorator and her floral skills were pure art. She could pick antiques and create vignettes that made our home seem like a cottage out of the pages of a fairy tale. Even when there was little to no budget, our holidays were Martha Stewart–worthy. For a few days anyway. Then she would sink in the quicksand of her depression and the house didn't get cleaned for incredibly long periods and a darkness settled over everything like the dust on the furnishings. There were times in my life when I thought, "She's going to be ok." They just never lasted. My mom was a beautiful, magical, heart-breaking disaster.

On top of being bipolar, she battled constant manic depression. So sadly, for a good portion of my life she was asleep. That taught me some not-so-good things. I learned I wasn't important or worthy enough for her to be awake. I struggled with loneliness and insecurity as a little girl. We didn't know which mom we would get on which day—the Fairy Godmother from Cinderella, complete with sparkles and sewing skills, or Sleeping Beauty. Everything in my life seemed either perfect or pitiful. There was no grey area. Even our meals depended on how Mama was feeling. They were either fabulous, southern feasts or nonexistent. I have a vague memory of eating empty ice cream cones for breakfast on the way to the bus stop. My grandmother took on the role as lunch packer in elementary school. Thank goodness because I was so terribly skinny. On top of enjoying a regularly balanced meal, I learned the art of gourmet lunch boxes. Think charcuterie, but instead of a wood serving tray it was nestled inside a metal Wonder Woman lunch box. (Squirrel: One time a little boy, stole my "Tid Bit" crackers and sharp cheddar slices, and I whooped the snot out of him in front of the class. Poor Timmy.)

Sometimes I wish I could go back and take care of my mom. Protect her. Shelter her from whatever heartache was inflicted on her when she was little, so that she could have had a good life. I look back on my time with her with a mixture of great love, anger, regret, and heartache all wrapped so tight that I can't separate them, like when you smash your Play-Doh colors together. Within the last few years, I have started to realize that I was both traumatized and neglected a large part of my childhood. It makes me sad. Maybe one of the reasons I didn't know it at the time, was because there were enough people around that I didn't realize how much mama wasn't. They did their best to help mask reality. That's the true hallmark of a southern family: gather close and hide the crap.

When my father wasn't working, he did his best to shelter us from our mom's meltdowns. I think he was mostly successful. Okay, maybe not. I remember shattered mirrors and whaling in the night. I had a close relationship with my dad, and I adored him. When he pulled in after work, I would literally run up our holly lined drive to hug him. Every. Single. Time. Even as a teenager. My father was a builder and I loved to go to work with him. (Squirrel: One time I ran through a freshly poured beach hotel sidewalk. And I got so many swats.) My dad seemed to always be accomplishing these big amazing projects. And I knew I wanted to build big amazing things too. He was not perfect. Far from it. Looking back, I think his constant worry for what others thought kept my mom from getting the help she needed. He also bullied her to try and get her to "act normal." Then there was the fighting...oy vey. My parents were either madly in love or engulfed in flames of anger. My dad helped turn a closet in my room into a reading nook with shelves. My mom helped me decorate it and make it cozy. It's where I hid when the battles would begin.

Another added hiccup in my childhood was the fact that I didn't look like any of my siblings. They all had dark hair and brown eyes. And they never let me forget it. My sisters had all but convinced me I was the milk man's baby, but I have my dad's strawberry blonde hair and grey eyes. Also, our milk man was a girl. And she delivered newspapers.

I'd be remiss if I did not include the cherries on top of my already distorted childhood...the prescription drug parade that marched through like Macy's on Thanksgiving. But instead of a huge Snoopy balloon, there was a giant Vicodin pill, and my parents held onto the strings for dear life. Those were the days when doctors just loved to give out painkillers. And my family happily accepted. I am not saying that my mom's mental illness and my dad's physically crippling arthritis were not legit reasons for medicinal help. I'm just saying the pharmaceutical companies were super generous with opioids and benzos in the eighties and nineties. This certainly didn't help improve my parent's child rearing skills or ability to budget.

I think the phrase beautiful disaster perfectly describes my first eighteen years. And let's just be real and admit that the following decade was just as shaky. It would be easy for me to use that part of my life as an excuse. An excuse to be bitter. An excuse to blame others. An excuse to hide. I think most of us can find legitimate reasons to be angry about things that have happened in our lives. Things we couldn't control. Hurt that was inflicted. Even the parents we were given.

Here's what I'm learning: None of that does any good. It just holds us back. It is impossible to see all that is ahead when our eyes are still trained on what's behind. And please don't think for a moment I am saying I have it all figured out. Because I am totally aware that I am still just fumbling through. But I know that every day I have to make a conscious decision to not allow where I had been to hold me back from where I want to go. And one of the things I had to do, was forgive my parents. Often. They did the best they could, with what they had, with what they knew, and with who they were. And when those skeletons of bitterness start to rise—and oh, friends, they do—I immediately put them back where they belong. Tacky clothes and all.

I also had to give myself permission to mourn for the little girl I was, and what she endured. In my head, she is still five. She is huddled in a beautifully decorated little closet wearing a frilly yellow dress from the first day of school. Her hair is a typical tangled mess, and her eyes are red-rimmed and filled with tears because she is so afraid. And I swoop in and hug her tight. So tight. I tell her that everything is going to be ok. Because one day she will conquer giants. She is destined for so much more. And she's about to create a fairy tale all her own.

When we process and deal with our baggage from the past, we make room for more. More connection. More happiness. More love and acceptance. If you're like me, your shoulders are tired of carrying all those unwanted suitcases filled with things you never even want to wear again. Maybe your childhood was fabulous, and your parents were great, but you had a teacher who said things to you that you still replay like an old dusty record to this day. Maybe it was friend, a coach, an uncle, a boyfriend. I don't know who is in your past, or how it affected you, but whatever it is... give yourself permission to deal with what you have been through. Cry. Get mad. Punch someone. No—don't do that last one. But please find someone you trust who you can talk with. A counselor, a mentor, a faith leader, a very wise friend. Someone. Because it's time to begin healing. It may take months. Most likely, years. But face it head-on. Get those tears out. And then wipe your face off, lift your head, and move forward. No more using it as a crutch or an excuse. Because your past does not define you—it simply prepares you.

CHAPTER 2

GRAPEVINES AND SERPENTS

Embracing the Way You're Wired

"An acorn can grow into an oak tree, but it cannot become a rose bush."

—*John Ortberg, The Me I Want to Be*

When I was in preschool, I used to roam our family's property while the other kids were at school. This was the late seventies, so parenting rules hadn't taken effect. With an eight-year gap between my younger brother and me, I was the only "little" running around the property for quite some time. When I was small, I just knew that our land was like the garden of Eden as they described it in Sunday School. I grew up in coastal Virginia where there were farms, and forests, AND the ocean. (Insert three sets of heart eyes.) Our family's property had ginormous fig trees, pear trees, pecan trees, grape vines, raspberry bushes, and wild apple trees, and the grown-ups wouldn't let me eat from any of them. As far as I knew, there were no talking snakes, so I didn't see a problem with tasting things. There was one particularly forbidden fruit that they would always shoo me away from. The big juicy southern muscadine grapes. They all but glowed on the vines…calling to me. Like little purple sirens.

One afternoon, I walked out to the backyard, and there was my grandmother, my aunts, and some older cousins all harvesting the grapes. They selfishly would use them to make jams and jellies and other such nonsense. I panicked at the thought that once again they would steal all the fruit for themselves. So, I did what any rational four-year-old would do. I put on my invisible cape and plotted how best to get one last taste. My plan: to run as fast as I could, grab a cluster, and continue without stopping until I was safely inside the fig tree by our outdoor bird house. It was foolproof. I would be invisible after all. So, I crouched under a large bush, my chin resting on my knees, leaves sticking out of my hair, barefoot, waiting for the perfect moment to spring into action. When the time came that it seemed no one was looking in my direction, I launched out of the bush like a tiny rocket. I ran towards the grape covered trellis, invisible cape flowing behind me, and I grabbed a handful of fat round grapes. I just had to make it to the hiding space before anyone noticed so I could enjoy the fruits of my labor. As I ran forward, I felt a slight tug and a pop. And then another tug and pop, and yet another. I turned around and saw that I had not grabbed just a cluster of grapes but an actual vine as well. And the further away I ran, the longer the vine became that trailed behind me. And then the yelling ensued. My cover was blown. Now, panic stricken, all I knew to do was run as fast as I could with the ten-foot grape vine trailing behind me like an angry serpent. Followed by six screamin' women.

Unfortunately, that was just the first of many, many escapades that would land me in trouble over the course of my life. Turns out, on top of my other gifts, God thought it would also be a good idea to bless me with a little thing we now call ADHD. It gave me superpowers, yes. But also questionable decision-making skills. When I was tiny, I was referred to as hard-headed, strong-willed, ornery, tenacious, and hyper. My report cards always had 3 boxes checked: excessive talking, inability to sit still, needs improvement. I was the poster child of "what were you thinking?" Not much has changed. Except now I don't think there's something inherently wrong with me. Albert Einstein has been attributed with saying, "Everybody is genius. But if you judge a fish by its ability to climb a tree, it will live its whole life believing it was stupid." I'm glad I finally realized I wasn't created to climb trees.

No childhood recap would be complete without the telling of the toad incident. I was three, maybe four. It was summertime for sure. I remember the sound of locusts, the smell of honeysuckle, and my mamas' wildflowers, particularly Black-Eyed Susans growing next to the sidewalk in front of our home. My dad had a glass of sun tea and he was sitting on the stairs. (Squirrel: My oldest sister used two cups of sugar when making her famous sun tea. Two cups y'all. I'm lucky I still have teeth.) My dad was sitting on our front porch carving an owl out of a block of wood. I wanted to help him. And I started having a temper tantrum when he wouldn't let me use the knife. So, to show him how mad I was, I grabbed a toad that was sitting nearby and smashed it on the ground right next to his well-worn Sperry topsider. Oh, Holy Hannah. Time stood still. That is one of the few times I recall as a child my dad being truly upset with me. After my well-deserved spanking he gave me a lecture on how we NEVER kill animals unless we plan to eat them. Then he made me eat the smashed toad. Ok, I'm just kidding. He didn't. But he did make me clean it up and give it a proper burial. And then he talked to me about the importance of nature and God's creatures. I cried and cried for the toad mama and her babies that now had no daddy to bring home food and a Christmas tree. To this day, I try to follow those lessons. Except with flies. They deserve to die.

It's easy to look back and find humor in my misadventures now. However, it seems that for a large part of my life I made things infinitely more difficult than they needed to be. I apparently have a bend, or a wiring per se, that leads me to the path less traveled…without a map. The really rocky one that has cliffs on both sides and bright red signs that warn "Do Not Enter." Did I mention I hate to ask for directions?

Now, as an adult I may not be stealing grapes or smashing toads but that certainly does not mean that some of my natural born tendencies don't still end with me in hot water. There is not a day that goes by that I don't think "Did I actually just say that?" Basically, I'm still four. I can't sit still, I talk too much, I come across brash, I don't always play well with others, and if you don't hand over the knife, there may be consequences.

Here's what I'm learning: Discovering more about myself and embracing how I am wired has played a pivotal role in helping me become more of who I want to be. We are all born with "a hitch in our giddy-up" in one way or another. I am not a medical professional, so I will not speak on genetic make-up or hereditary predispositions. But I don't know anyone who is perfect. We all have issues. And I for one will tell you that life seems to be better when I embrace exactly who I am, warts and all. It's a daily choice to not allow those things to hold me back or keep me from where I want to go.

What are some character traits that seem to land you in hot water, or set you apart as different or weird? Once we acknowledge these traits, it's easier to make sure they don't get in the way of where we want to go. As a matter of fact, what's even more amazing is we can use those very things to empower us. I've found that it is these traits that, when used wisely, are our biggest assets and allow us to make our mark in this world. When we embrace the way we are wired, we stop using our energy to hide or change, and we start putting that energy toward what we are destined to accomplish, those dreams in our hearts that feel inextricably linked to us.

My hard-headedness and proclivity to forge my own path, even if there is a perfectly placed cobblestone right in front of me, has allowed me to— with much effort and many trials— to accomplish things that I never would have dreamed were possible. My design company, our So. Bell & Co. Fall Marketplace, and my art line are all perfect examples of this.

Sure, sometimes these same traits may land us in hot water, but even in the chaos, we will become more of who we were created to be, and I think that's really important to remember. Seek wisdom in these areas, love others as well as you can, and remember that it's ok if we sometimes upset the apple cart as we make our mark on the world. We just have to be sure to set it up right again when were finished.

CHAPTER 3

ART SCHOOLS AND GOAT PARTS

When the World Says No, Tune It Out

"Rejection doesn't have to mean you aren't good enough; it often just means the other person failed to notice what you have to offer."

—*Ash Sweeney*

My first memory of being an artist was roaming door to door in our neighborhood selling my goods like a pint-sized peddler. I was probably five or six years old. I would glue sticks, leaves, and berries to notebook paper in a variety of sticky, shapeless designs to create collages. I also had an entire line of crudely painted rocks. You could have your choice of either for a dollar. Which would be like ten bucks today, so I was sort of a scam artist also. But my mom convinced me they were beautiful, and my dad thought it was a great business idea. My poor neighbors.

When I was in second grade, I won first place for my rendition of "The Fruit Bowl" done in chalk pastels. I vaguely remember the winner's art being displayed at some public location. (Airport maybe? Local jail?) I received a cheap navy-blue ribbon that my parents treated like a Nobel

Prize. They kept telling people about it and introducing me like I was famous. "This is our little Bird, the artist." What?! Me?! A famous Artist you say? I equate this to the scene in Harry Potter when Hagrid say's "You're a Wizard Harry!" The only obvious differences were that I was not British, a boy, or a wizard. And the school was considerably less magical than Hogwarts

I continued with my art career through elementary school and could not wait to take my first real art class in seventh grade. I was pretty sure I would be better than the other students because I had a blue ribbon.

In eighth grade I applied to Hogwarts…I mean art school. The school requested all submittals be in a portfolio. So, my dad and I researched what a real portfolio looked like and then he took me to buy one from the office supply store. It was large and black, and I still remember it smelling richly of new plastic. Based on the information in the packet I received, I filled my shiny portfolio full of all that they requested. Examples of pencil drawings, pen and ink, watercolor, acrylic, etc.

I remember pulling up to an office at the front of a building that looked entirely too tired to host creative people or wizards. I was ushered into a poorly lit room that smelled of moldy wood. The walls were lined with dark Formica tables and you could see the dust motes floating in the air through the tiny sliver of sunlight desperate to enter the dingy space. I laid my work neatly all along the tables. Three gentlemen walked in. They looked eerily like one another with heads in various stages of baldness and graying beards. They slowly filed past my art with constipated looks on their faces while making a variety of harrumph and hmmmm noises. I felt the sudden urge to grab all my work and hide it. I was a kid, and my soul was laying wide open on an ugly table and it was being judged. After a series of vague diagnoses and encouragement to try other mediums, they suggested I develop my craft and try again the following year. I was crushed. And maybe a wee bit mad. I remember a quiet car ride home only punctuated by my sniffles and my father's ignored words of encouragement.

But those emotions did not last long. Have I mentioned yet that I'm hard-headed? Also, I come from a long line of people who don't know when they are supposed to quit. Besides, I had a freaking blue ribbon. So, in my little rebel heart I gave that school the proverbial bird that day and decided I was just too much of an artist for their dusty ole school anyway. New plan: I would take all the art electives in high school that I could, and those bald men would be sorry they turned me down when I became really famous. (I'm not dramatic at all.)

I took art in the ninth and tenth grade. Art I and Art II. I loved it. I was pretty sure I was good. The teacher complimented me often. Towards the end of my junior year she encouraged me to apply for AP art as a senior. And you guessed it! I was a first-round pick. Ok. That's a lie. I told you I was dramatic. I didn't actually get in. And I cannot exactly recollect why. But I remember having that "not worthy" feeling again. And the message that I was not a real artist was getting louder. It seems as though the "unworthy" and "not good enough" feelings stick to your soul like tar on your shoes in the summer. And the layers get thicker and thicker.

After high school I wrote and illustrated a children's book. After lots of letters and lots of silence, I finally received one response. Dear Sir or Madam, your illustrations were not of professional level that we prefer. I don't even remember what they said about the words. So I packed the whole thing up and placed it in a box in my attic. Not because I was quitting. I'm just going to make a big comeback when I'm sixty. Then they'll be sorry.

As the years progressed, those would not be the only doors that were shut on me as an artist. But I continued to create anyway, because I knew in my heart it was what I was born to do. I hustled through multiple pointless jobs and college courses over the next decade, but I was always creating something. Not always something good, mind you. My list of additional art fails includes but are not limited to:

- When I lived in Hawaii (yes, we'll come back to this shortly), I painted the cutest tiny little ocean murals on the sides of jars that contained sand from the local beach. I had them for sale along with a few other handcrafted items in front of a friend's house where we put together a tiny arts and crafts show. They were completely adorable. Which was why I was utterly perplexed that I didn't sell even a single one. That is until I solved the mystery two years later while cleaning my garage. I was taking the entire box to a local goodwill, along with some other donations, and noticed one little error in my execution. On the backside of all the jars I spelled Hawaii "Hawii." Oh yes I did. On all twenty-four jars. And no one had said a word.

- When I first moved to Texas, I was really hoping to find work as an artist. I knew it would take a while but felt confident the news of my blue ribbon would get out. Seriously though, the extra income would come in handy while single mommin' (we'll come back to this too) so I was willing to take whatever jobs came my way. Which is why I was elated when another local designer contacted me to do a commissioned piece. She said it would be a painting of someone's prized goat applied to metal. Ok. Weird but whatever. It pays. She let me know she would deliver the metal to my house with a picture of the goat. When she dropped off the metal, she forgot to mention it would be in the shape of a goat. An anatomically correct goat. I called a friend of mine that night crying. When she asked what was going on, I blurted out, "I'm painting goat balls that's what's going on!" And to this day, painting that goat's testicles has been the low point of my career.

- I discovered through a project at our local church that murals were basically just like really big canvases. I started painting murals. Lots of them. And it was great extra income. I also figured out that murals were not that difficult. It was the writing on the murals that was my issue. Along with misspelling two kids' names in their own bedrooms, I spelled rejoice, "rejoyce" in my friend's bathroom.

- And finally, my *piece de resistance*: Tiny Noah. I was hired by someone who is now one of my dear friends to paint a full room scene of Noah's Ark with the all the animals. Easy peezy. I can paint giant animals all day long. So, I filled the walls with animals of every species, boo and bae. Ginormous, beautiful, detailed animals. And these were not cartoon animals. This was a legit realistic mural. No coloring book animals here, folks. You want that? Go visit the dentist's office. I was making magic. Until it came time to paint Noah. After about an hour I quickly realized that I could not paint Noah to save my life. And don't ask me why. He just kept looking like a man in drag. Which would be fine in the right setting. But not in a kid's room in a mural depicting a Bible story. (To this day, painting people is my kryptonite. I am horrible.) I started sweating profusely at the thought of telling this homeowner that I was unable to paint the "Noah" in her Noah and his Ark mural. But then I came up with a stroke of genius. One word: Perspective. I start painting hills in the background. And then I painted a couple extra-large animals in the foreground to really play up the depth. And finally, at the top of one of the highest mountains I painted an ark about a foot tall, with teeny tiny little animals climbing towards it, two by two, getting smaller and smaller. And there keeping watch, just to the left was Noah. All 1.25 inches of him. When I brought the homeowner, Heather, in for the big reveal, she was speechless. Her breath literally caught in her throat. The ten-foot rainbow sweeping two walls was magnificent. She told me how beautiful it all was. She even commented on the lifelikeness of the sheep and how soft their fur looked. And then she asked the dreaded question, "Where's Noah?" I respond by pointing my finger in a vague direction, and said over there by the sheep, without making eye contact. "Where?" She says. "Right there," I respond. So, I walk over and point to him. "See, right here next to his ark." She stared in silence with her mouth slightly gaping open. Shamelessly, I gave her a huge hug and told her how honored I was that she was so happy. Two decades later, we still crack up about it.

Here's what I'm learning: Ultimately, your success is defined by you and not the world. Did I ever get into art school? Nope. Did I ever land the cover of Boston Art Magazine? Nope. Did I ever get hired to illustrate a book? No again. However, was I able to contribute significantly to our family's income while raising my boys as a single mama slinging paint? Yes. Do I now own my own interior design company where I am often asked to paint custom art pieces for clients? Yes. Is my art in multiple State buildings, including two law libraries? I have no idea how, but yes. Do I have pieces in other countries? Oddly enough, yes. Did I finally launch my own line of prints? Yessiree Bob! And I am so excited! And, even bigger than all of that, I have made some of the most amazing lifelong friendships through my art. That's my biggest success. I feel like that's pretty good for the artist who wasn't supposed to be. And one of my most valuable lessons is that I decide what my success is defined as. And so do you.

Each time we ignore the "no's," we win. Each time someone tells us we can't do something, and we do it anyway, we succeed. Each time we are too stubborn, too hardheaded, or too head strong to quit...that's our accomplishment. This is about more than just achieving or failing. It's about moving forward and doing life our way. On our terms. Not someone else's.

We can't look to others to tell us what we aren't capable of, because they don't know us—not fully. They can't see our full potential, our drive, our gumption, our courage, our grit. We must follow those things rather than the opinions of others who—despite how they may act—do not know everything. We all have a blue ribbon or two tucked away somewhere that we may need to break out on occasion to remind us of our greatness, when the world shouts otherwise.

I'd love to say art is the only area of my life where I have been told I couldn't do something. But that would be untrue. I have also been told that I couldn't write books, be a designer, or build homes. I was told that I wouldn't be able to maintain normal activity levels because of a degenerative disease, and that I wouldn't be able to raise successful multi-racial sons as a single white woman. And my response to all of it, "Oh yeah? Watch me."

CHAPTER 4

POPS AND TARTS

You are Worthy

"Self-worth comes from one thing—thinking that you are worthy."
—*Wayne Dyer*

When you are a young girl who grows up with a mama who sleeps more than she's awake and a dad who buries himself in work to avoid reality, it doesn't take long for you to go in search of what's missing elsewhere.

I think I mentioned before that I often looked like a street urchin in my elementary school years. There were days I was best described as an orphan from a Charles Dickens novel. But not every day. Some days when mom had the energy, or my grandmother stepped in, I looked quite cute. And I became aware that people treated me differently. By fourth grade I was basically responsible for myself when my grandmother wasn't there. So, I tried my best to look like everyone else with what I had to choose from. By junior high my father's businesses were very successful so there was a lot more money—and a lot less parents. I often think this is the worst position you could place a child in. My mother was busy drowning herself with everything she could find, and my dad was making out checks in order to buy affection. My friends lovingly called him Pops, and he gave them money when he gave me money. He didn't mind paying for everything either. I look back and realize he thought he was doing good by us. But I'm not sure any 12-year-old needs $200 sunglasses and a pocket full of cash.

My dad was more concerned with outward appearances than he was with reality. He pushed me hard in school, and I soon began to realize that if I was excellent then he paid attention. And I began to equate my worth with how much I could achieve. (Sadly, one of my greatest regrets as a parent is creating a new generation of overachievers. But I now have the wisdom to make sure my sons know their worth does not lie with their accomplishments. It's never too late to break false beliefs.)

With MIA parents and money, it was easy to get into trouble. This was also the period of my life where I was starting to get noticed by boys. And I liked it very much. It turned out I was not the ugly duckling. I started playing soccer and I took dance classes, and my body continued to change. I learned to dress to get attention and to shamelessly flirt. I was a tart and so were my friends. (Squirrel: One time me and three of my friends were walking down Atlantic Ave next to the boardwalk in Virginia Beach acting like stupid teenagers. We were all clad in string bikinis and side ponytails. A car full of guys in a convertible Shelby mustang drove by, catcalling. So, we started waving, and giggling, and generally acting like ditzes. Not paying a lick of attention, I ran smack into a steel light pole and got waylaid to the ground. I laugh about it now. Little hussy.)

I was more than just boy crazy. My entire identity was wrapped up in what I looked like and who was paying attention to me. I felt empty all the time and desperate to feel worthy of someone's attention. My friends and I went to a dance club every weekend for kids under 18. I became obsessed with being the best dancer and the prettiest girl there. But I was never either. And it did not matter how much attention I received—it was never enough.

It's almost physically painful to be sharing this. This pattern only increased and became more dangerous as my high school years progressed. I went to parties, I acted like a tart, and treated myself like I had no value.

My junior year of high school, my dad and my mom separated. Even in all the instability, at least their togetherness was a constant. But when they broke apart, so did I. My level of heartbreak and anger caused me to spiral out of control. My rebellion further escalated culminating in a pregnancy my senior year of high school. My parents reunited sometime during my pregnancy. But my father did not talk to me until after my son was born.

I am not sure fathers truly understand the roles they play in their daughter's lives. I stopped blaming my dad a long time ago. But I have no doubt that, had he been more protective, more engaged, and more aware of the impact he could have made, I may have missed a few of the potholes on the streets of my youth.

Sadly, my story is far too common. In 2014 I started working with a group of girls in our community. They were going into their ninth-grade year of high school. And over the next four years until they graduated, at least half of them shared similar stories with different details. The commonality always seemed to come back to the desire to be loved and to feel worthy. And it seems no matter how old we get, the desire is the same. I was well into my thirties before I finally stopped chasing after the things that I thought would finally make me feel good enough, pretty enough, worthy enough, or accomplished enough to deserve love.

I've noticed that some people hide their desperation to find worth better than others. Especially as they age. Often, they can even come off looking noble. Have you ever met anyone who volunteers for every opportunity available? They are room mom, PTA president, hold seats on multiple boards, and take a meal to every new mom and sick person in town? How about the mom who does everything for her kids? Packs gourmet lunches, makes breakfast every morning, obsesses over their clothes, runs their homework to school if they forget it, stalks their kids' teachers, makes handmade Halloween costumes, and acts as a personal agent for all their athletic and extracurricular activities? What about the career super woman? Have you met her? She works nights and weekends. She accepts nothing but perfection. She is strong, tenacious, and can multitask like no one you have ever met. Her phone is always ringing, and she will not stop until she's the best in her field. And oh yeah—she's too busy for you. Have you ever met anyone obsessed with the way they look? They exercise constantly, they go to all the social events, everything they wear looks cute, and they wouldn't dare miss their nail appointment. What about homemaker Barbie? Her house is Instagram-worthy, she hosts perfect parties, she bakes gourmet desserts to post on Facebook, and she owns an "I Love Martha" t-shirt.

I could keep going but I think you get the picture. There is an infinite number of ways that we try to convince ourselves that we are good enough, worthy enough, and deserving enough of love. How do I know this? Because after I realized that a man could never make me feel that worthy, I turned to everything listed above. Those descriptions above are descriptions of me at one point or another in my life. And can I just tell y'all, I ended up real damn tired, and my self-worth was still missing.

Obviously, none of the things I listed are bad things. It's obsessively doing them for the wrong reasons that's the issue. Women have perfected the art of doing the right thing for the wrong reason.

Here's what I'm learning: It's never too late to course-correct. The race isn't over until we are buried and gone. So how do we do that? By accepting that we are good enough, worthy enough, and deserving enough just how we are. There is nothing we can do or say or be that makes us any more valuable than we already are. And you have to believe it. If not, you will keep chasing.

And if you share a similar faith as me, then we know we are worthy, because HE says so. Ephesians 2:10. 1 Peter 2:9. Psalm 139:14. I live my life differently now. All those things I did to make myself feel worthy are now just wonderful additions to a life well loved. I work out differently, I volunteer differently, cook differently, but most important…I love my people differently. And it's beautiful because everything is more enjoyable when you do it because you want to do it, not because you have to prove yourself. Do I still post my cake pops on IG? Oh, absolutely. But not because I'm looking for value—it's because I want to give value. Do I still cook for my friends? Heck yeah! But because I want to bless them, and my feelings are not crushed if my etouffee gags them a little. I don't have this down completely. I still have to check my own motives sometimes, but I can promise you, life feels so much better.

I don't know what your "thing" is. Or if you're like me, you have many, many "things." But I highly encourage you to examine your life. What are you chasing? What are you trying to fill holes with? Start to look at what motivates you. And then make the decision to remind yourself every single day that those things are not who you are, and they don't decide your worth. Write it on your mirror, tape it to your dashboard, pin it to your memo board. Because sister, You Are Worthy. Just as you are.

CHAPTER 5

UNPLANNED BABIES AND BICYCLES

The Wisdom of Walking Away

"Sometimes walking away has nothing to do with weakness, and everything to do with strength. We walk away not because we want others to realize our worth and value, but because we finally realize our own.

—Robert Tew

After I became unexpectantly pregnant with my first son, the mixed-up values ingrained in me from my father triggered the belief that I needed to make the relationship work with the baby's father. Not just make it work, but somehow, I needed to succeed. I had to. Failure was not an option. I now equate this with trying to build a racecar with an empty toolbox. All the tenacity in the world ain't gonna make the engine run.

When Mr. Bell (that's what I call him) and I got married, we were both young and broken, and he had some very unstable personality traits to say the least. Still, the little trooper (substitute idiot) that I am, I kept going. I am not a quitter or all that other B.S. I was a mess and had never learned to be in a healthy relationship. I was quite likely a horrible wife. And I will be the first to admit that I made a million mistakes during my first marriage.

The first year was rough (as well as the subsequent years). I remember being seven months pregnant, newly married, and still trying to learn to work a stove. (Oh how I regret not being in the kitchen on the occasions when my mama actually cooked. She was amazing.) The first time I attempted spaghetti, Mr. Bell had a few extra ugly remarks. This was my first glimpse into the mental and emotional abuse that would permeate our entire marriage. So, after a few more unkind critiques, he finished with, "If you knew how to cook, you would know that a cooked noodle will stick on the wall when it's done." Oh really? When I was done the entire kitchen was covered floor to ceiling with spaghetti.

I can still conjure up the emptiness I felt during those years. I looked to fill my brokenness in every wrong way. I built walls upon walls. I was a broken kid, with a kid, trying to find my value. So, what did I need to improve the situation? Another kid. Specifically, a boy. I'm not kidding. My rationale was that Andy would have a brother (I had already named him Alex), and I would have a little family. What more would I need? And so, I got pregnant and had a boy…and named him Alex.

Mr. Bell was in the military, so we lived in multiple places and he was rarely around. Both by choice and military directive. He left multiple times during those years, which worked out great for me because I had my little family and I loved being a mom. Many of those years were a complete blur because I was mostly just terrified when he was home, so the less time we had to deal with him the better. I look back and understand one of the reasons I was able to hold on for so long is because he wasn't usually around. For the most part, I was a single mom from the moment I gave birth to our first son. Unfortunately, sometimes, he was around. Those were dark times. I felt like if I could just shelter the boys from their dad, then it would be okay. Sadly, I can think of more than one occasion when the boys were little when I barricaded us in a bedroom. Praying for daylight.

Even now, as wave upon wave of memories come back, I think *what the hell was wrong with me? Why did I stay?* I have to remind myself that I was just a teenager, with no self-worth and no idea how I would financially take care of two little boys. Weeks after Alex was born, we were sent to Hawaii. That time in my life was a mixture of amazing happiness, intense fear, and deep shame. I finally went to a counselor and told them about the years of the abuse, after an incident involving gasoline. They brought him in and documented everything. I hated being thought of as a victim. I don't remember the consequences, but it seems things were less volatile after that.

When we were transferred to Connecticut, we were surrounded by the best neighbors ever. I still love them dearly. I was getting better at learning how to keep the explosions to a minimum when Mr. Bell was around, and hiding them when they happened. And he was mostly gone. But I was also getting older, and less afraid. Less afraid of him, less afraid of parenting on my own. And now I had our third baby boy, Alan. And I knew I didn't want the children or myself to live this way anymore. So, after about a year in Connecticut, I decided enough was enough. Myself, a six-year-old, a four-year-old, and an infant, left Connecticut and moved back home to be near my sister on the Outer Banks of North Carolina.

I want to clarify that me and the boys didn't have a joyless existence. To know my personality is to know that is impossible. Broken or not, I will make the best of the situation. The boys and I enjoyed every single day we could. We had lots of homes and adventures, and a couple of places still hold a special place in my heart. We spent lots of time building sandcastles on the beaches in Hawaii. We explored the trails and the tropical parks. We went to aquariums and kid's museums. In Connecticut, the boys started school, so I was able to be involved in their classrooms. I loved PTA and being room mom. We went apple picking in the fall and sledding in the winter. We took nature walks and packed picnics. I made homemade games, and we baked, and crafted all the time. We lived in libraries wherever we landed. And we made lots of great friends. Many that I keep up with to this day. I'm not sure any of them knew the level of fear that hovered over our home.

Once we made it back home to Carolina, the happy days were more of a norm. I worked part time gigs. I did some side decorating and painted a couple of murals. And my sister and I did everything together with our kids. We finally had some peace. Poor as church mice, but happy. One Christmas we didn't even have enough for a Christmas tree, so we cut our own down and decorated it with handmade ornaments. And guess what? It was my favorite tree to this day.

This is where you may question my sanity. After a year on our own in North Carolina, Mr. Bell reached out. He was convinced he was a changed man—he had been getting help, and he was ready to give being a dad 100 percent. He asked for a second chance, not with me but with the boys. And my greatest wish for my sons was to have a dad in their life who loved them. And I could see that they were desperate to have him around. He said he was moving home to Texas and asked if I would consider taking the boys there. And against my entire family's protestations, and my better judgment, I agreed. We moved from an island in North Carolina to the desert in West Texas. Holy crap.

This is where it gets tricky. The boys and I moved to Texas. But Mr. Bell didn't. Yes, you read that right. Andy had just turned eight. Alex was five. Alan was eighteen months. We loaded up all of our belongings, left everything and everyone we knew in Carolina, and shortly after, Mr. Bell dropped us off at his mom's. He was supposed to go back and settle his affairs on the coast and then return to Texas. But he didn't come back. At first, we didn't know anything was going on. He just kept vaguely saying it was going to take longer for him to move. And he blamed it on the military.

I was getting sick of the excuses and it didn't take much longer for me to realize he was not coming. The situation at his mother's was beyond toxic. So, the boys and I quickly moved out of his mom's and into an efficiency hotel for a bit, and then moved into the smallest crappiest trailer you could ever imagine. I was working at a department store and it was all I could afford. We were all but starving. During our brief stay at his mother's I quickly figured out where Mr. Bell's special personality traits came from. His mother had an interesting assortment of unpleasant character traits. And I learned that he never knew his father, according to his mother. But apparently, he was part Asian and African-American and he died when Mr. Bell was six, never acknowledging him. (By the way, if your brain is swirling a bit and trying to figure out the various races that make up my children, good luck. I don't even know. It's too many to count. Whatever the combination, it was magic.)

When I realized Mr. Bell was not coming to Texas, I was too proud and too stubborn to admit to my family that they had been right. So, in a town where we knew no one, I did the only thing I knew to do. Pulled up my big girl britches and made it work. There was many a time I didn't know where our next meal was coming from, but somehow, we survived. And the crappy little trailer became a crappy little apartment, and then a less crappy little house, and so on.

The boys and I lived on our own in Texas for a couple years, but Mr. Bell did eventually come moseying back to town. He wanted to try to be a dad again. He didn't have a place to stay, so we tried to cohabitate for a while, so he could be near the kids. We had a house, he got a job, and I even dragged him to church and small group for some time. All while pretending things were perfectly normal. Not admitting to anyone the dysfunction of it all. But he got worse again. A lot worse. I have tried to refrain from sharing too many details because I do not want to dishonor how far he has come almost fifteen years later. But for the sake of showing how hardheaded I am, let me add the next sentence. When I finally came to the realization that he was just not willing to get his life straight, he was not only extremely unstable, he was unemployed, intoxicated, had multiple random girlfriends threatening me, and was sleeping on the couch that I had paid for with my hard-earned money, under a roof I was also paying for every single month. So yes, I finally gave him the boot. Forever. And I filed for divorce. I was no longer afraid. But I felt like a failure.

During this time, there were threats to burn down my little single mom house. And multiple unstable women (Mr. Bells friends) were calling me as well. So, we had to go stay with some friends for a few days and we took mini hotel vacations until things settled. Eventually a restraining order and court papers made him go away. I was granted full custody of the boys and he had court supervised visitation twice a month, which he never went to.

Yes. I'm hard-headed. I just wanted what was best for my boys. I wanted to believe that Mr. Bell had changed and that he was going to give parenting 100 percent of his effort. So it may sound crazy how long I was with him, but it's hard to fully wrap your head around abuse when you're still in it and when you're trying to match up what you want reality to be with actual reality. Now that I'm in my forties, I look back and know that I did the best I could with what I knew and with where I was. And I must give myself a little grace.

Do you want to know the craziest thing about my feelings in all of it? I had more or less always been a single mom on some level even during the few years Mr. Bell and I actually received mail at the same address. And during the later years, I was the financial provider. And yet, once the divorce was finalized I kind of panicked. Because what if I couldn't provide for my little family? And I doubted myself. The good news is, not all the values my parents instilled in me were completely jacked. My mom taught me to love everyone, regardless of where they come from. She taught me to treasure the beauty in our world. She taught me to make the best of bad situations. And she taught me to embrace my creative heart. My dad taught me to say I love you often. He taught me that stealing is absolutely never ok. He taught me to stand up for the underdogs. And he taught me to work hard and fight hard. So that's what I did. That's what we did. We lived those lessons, through the good and the bad, we worked hard and found joy in our life.

Being a single mom was absolutely the hardest thing I ever did. And I don't have enough pencils to write out all the ways I screwed up. But there was so much joy also. And it shaped me in every good way. Being a single parent makes you tough. It teaches you patience and self-control. You learn to have a compassionate heart, and to thank God for every single thing you have. (Squirrel: For years we received no form of financial support from my ex. So, when we received that first check, a whopping $300—yes, that was for three kids—I told the boys we could put it towards new bikes. We went to one of the local big box stores and I told the boys they could have any bike they wanted. After we had checked out, we walked toward the front and the woman checking receipts cheered "Woohoo, who's birthday?" My middle son replied, equally as loud, "No one's, we finally got child support!" Did I mention being a single mom gives you a huge dose of humility also?)

Here's what I'm learning: It's easy to confuse stubbornness and perseverance. They are not the same thing. And let's be honest, I am good at both. Sometimes you must be smart enough to know when to walk away. It's not failure. It's wisdom. It's not quitting. It's believing in yourself, believing you're worth more. Every ounce of me is a fighter. But sometimes the best thing to do is to know when to take the gloves off. Go back to your corner. Clean your wounds and give them time to heal. Because I promise you, there will come a time when you need to fight again. There will be a reason for you to pick those gloves back up and stare that opponent down. And when that time comes you have to be ready.

CHAPTER 6

SUPERHEROES AND VILLAINS

Knowing When It's Time to Fight

There are pros and cons to single parenting. The con is: if you screw up the kids, it's all your fault. But if you succeed, well then, you have a shot at raising Superman. It's impossible to discuss every obstacle of parenting. Much less the added challenges of single parenting, broke parenting, or parenting children who look nothing like you. So, I thought maybe I would pick three things that impacted us as a family on different levels. One for each kid. And let me add that challenges are as individual as humans are. So, these are our stories, told from my perspective, about us.

ANDY

Let's start with the oldest and navigating the waters of color. When you have blonde hair, blue eyes, and fair skin, and your children have black hair, brown eyes, and brown skin, it sometimes confuses people. I have said the phrases, "no I'm not the babysitter" and "no they're not adopted" more times than I can count. At playgrounds and at school, I had to answer the question "Why are your kids black?" and they had to answer, "Why is your mom white?" When the boys were feeling especially mischievous in the grocery store and I would tell them they couldn't have something, they thought it was funny to announce, "This woman is not our mom, help!" So, nervous onlookers watched as a crazy eyed white lady quickly left the store with three small black boys, wondering whether they should call the police. It's funny now. But by their third and fourth time, I learned to lean over and whisper, "I will whoop you in the bathroom." And that usually ended it.

I will not go through every single instance of racism we have experienced as a family because I believe mostly people are good. Just misinformed. And that more comments come from curiosity than maliciousness. I also believe that when you look for hate, you find it. So, I choose to look for joy. Most of the ugly instances occurred before the boys and I landed in Texas. There is just something about West Texas and the people here that embraced who we are. Almost from the moment we landed, they declared we were part of the community, and with that came the love and loyalty that Texas is known for. In many ways, from our church to the schools to the sports teams, we were in a bit of a bubble. This is not to say we did not deal with ignorant people, but overall, we were wholly accepted by our community. Most of the comments were from well-meaning friends, who didn't realize that their comments were, hmm…let's just say, not well thought out. The boy's white friends would say things like "You are the whitest black guy I have ever met." And their black friends would say things like "Why are you acting like a white guy?" It was as if the world just wanted to shove them away in a specific file folder but there was no appropriate label. My kids were the ones who checked the "other" box. I will never, in a million years, pretend to know everything they have battled in this world, because I do not live in their skin. But my mama's heart still hurts with them.

Although my children are multiracial, they identify as black. I'm guessing it's because of the way their father looks, and maybe even because that's the way the world sees them. Either way, it's how they see themselves. As for me…well I'm prejudiced. I just see the most beautiful children in the world that are created perfectly the way God designed them.

There was a reason why God gave me Andy first. He was perfectly designed to help lead his brothers. In many ways the oldest child is the pioneer—they take the uncharted paths, cutting through the jungle, taking the first hits for the family. That requires a lot of empathy. And that's my Andy. First of all, it's like he feels everything more than the average person. If he's happy, multiply it by ten. If he's sad, multiply it by ten. Frustrated, joyful, angry, etc. Some people would miss the gift in this. But I don't. I am sure society would have a label for him. I just call him "son." It gives him the ability to connect with others in the deepest of ways. He has an enormous amount of empathy. It's a superpower. Those deep emotions make him extremely loyal and aware of other's needs. He is basically going to be the best girl dad ever. But it also helped equip him for the special challenges that life would hand him as the oldest in a multiracial family.

He is also an intellectual and a thinker. And he has the inability to give up. Which is his other superpower. And his kryptonite. His stubbornness is like granite. When I say he has the inability to give up, I'm not exaggerating. When he was two, he touched a hot light bulb on a lamp and burnt his finger. I heard him say "ow," and I responded "That is hot, don't touch." He looked at the light bulb and touched it again. This time he yelled. And I grabbed his hand and held it and said "No no. Hot. Don't touch it." The moment I let go, he looked at me and then touched it again. This time he started crying. I remember in that moment thinking, *this is the most stubborn child alive. He's going to do something amazing one day. If he doesn't get himself blown up.* Then I moved the lamp.

It's that stubborn streak that made him perfect to be the oldest. He loves hard and doesn't back down. We need more people like that in this world. This was especially true when we dealt with our first real hatred when

Andy was a freshman in high school. He was dating a sweet blonde hair, blue eyed girl who played the same sports as him. But her parents were not just ignorant. They were ignorant racists. And just so you know, that is not a word I use lightly. Our culture seems to throw it around like a frisbee, or a weapon. And no longer gives it the importance it deserves. But in the case of these people, it's absolutely accurate. The words and judgment that Andy had to endure were not okay. No human should ever have to deal with that kind of hate simply because of the color God blessed them to be. This particular family was lucky my son has the precious heart he does. Because he would not let me react or get involved. He was afraid it would just cause more problems for the young lady. You guys know I wanted to whoop the snot out of that hideous mother and father. Don't mess with my children. Oh my goodness, the anger it evokes just typing this. I would like to take a moment to apologize for calling them names, but I will have to do that in my next book. I'm still too mad. I hope and pray there comes a day when the color of one's skin is no longer a reason to pass judgment. But until it does, if you mess with my family...it's on.

Because my personality and Andy's are so similar, we have had a long history of epic battles. We both have necessary and unnecessary scars. But it takes a fighter, an overcomer, and someone who doesn't give up to deal with racism. And his combination of empathy and perseverance is what will empower him to love hard in difficult situations, especially where color is concerned. And that's a very good thing. Because he now has a child who looks very different from him as well. And it will take all of his strength, tenacity, and most importantly empathy to be a black man raising his tiny, fair skinned, blue eyed little girl. He will have to endure the looks. The questions. And the ignorance. But he was created for this. And that sweet Marley girl will be well protected and well understood by a dad who has been purely equipped for the job. He was raised up for this. And I am so glad I have been blessed with a front row seat to watch those two change the world.

Here's what I'm learning: We have all been created to overcome certain challenges. And we have each had causes placed on our hearts that we are to fight for. And we haven't been sent in to battle unequipped. Often what society sees as a setback is actually a superpower. A beautiful tool that will help us win against the villains we will face. Villains of hate, judgment, ignorance, racism, and injustice. Andy was given a heart for the underdogs and God has equipped him for battle. There will be times, as a family, when we need to stand up for what we believe is right. But we don't always have to be looking for a fight either. I don't want our family to spend our lives looking for the villains. I would rather we keep our eyes out for the helpers, the victors, the superheroes. Call it naïve. Call it denial. But we will ultimately find what we are seeking. And I want us to find the good stuff.

Up next: the middle child and behavioral challenges.

ALEX

In the spring of '99 when Alex was about three and a half, before we had an official diagnosis, we already knew that he was wired uniquely. There was a time in Connecticut when my neighbor came to my door and told me to come quickly because Alex was about to jump out of his second story bedroom window. I ran outside to the front of the house and there was Alex, perched like a corn drunk crow on the windowsill wearing a bicycle helmet and positioned to leap. I was, at this point, somewhat used to Alex's alarming behavior, but nevertheless I yelled like a crazy woman and asked him what he thought he was doing. He replied slowly (like a parent explaining something to a child) and confidently that he was going to jump out of the window…but not to worry because he was wearing his helmet. Oh. Ok then. After many other "adventures," a doctor told me Alex had grandiose sense of accomplishment. He essentially believed he was indestructible. And that was just the beginning.

But let me rewind the film a bit. When Alex was born, he cried. And well, never stopped. At least through his toddler years. I was regularly taking him to our doctor because I knew this was more than colic. When he was about two and a half, I told the doctor I felt like he was not behaving quite as he should. His temper tantrums were frequent, explosive, and inconsolable. I explained that I had once complimented a picture he was coloring, and he began to scream and rip it up with his pencil. I told the doctor we could tell Alex we were heading to Disney World and he would react with hysterics. Taking him out in public was often nerve racking because you never knew how he would react. Loud noises terrified him, blinking lights on our Christmas tree were a no-no, and Katy, bar the door if his socks were misaligned. He was miserable, and I felt helpless. As I sat there further explaining his behavioral issues, I got the strong impression the doctor was not really listening to me. When I was finished, he suggested I look into a parenting class. (Yes, I had the briefest thought of slapping him upside his head. But I exercised my self-control muscles.) However, since I had already taken two parenting classes and read countless books, I decided to see another doctor. I knew without a doubt that my precious child was struggling internally. And it broke my heart. There were brief moments during the day when he seemed to be a completely happy rambunctious little boy, so I knew there was hope. And I was not going to stop until I figured out what was going on. (Mamas, when you know in your heart your child needs help, keep searching until you find it. Because you are right. And everyone else can kiss your…grits.)

Alex was three and a half when I found (in my opinion) one of the best child psychologists in Connecticut and made another appointment. (The boys' dad was military at the time, so we had great insurance.) Their initial hunch was early onset bipolar disorder, but they wanted to spend time with Alex and thoroughly evaluate him for an extended period of time. The emotions during that time were overwhelming. Mainly I tried to figure out what I was doing wrong. During those months we went through behavioral modification training with the counselor. We also saw the psychiatrist. I inhaled the reading material they would send home and practiced all the techniques we learned. There were no immediate major behavior changes, but we saw glimpses of progress. His final diagnosis was a very extreme case of ADHD that included Sensory Perception Disorder, Opposition Defiance Disorder, and a few other minor diagnoses. I was relieved to hear that he did not have bipolar disorder, but still overwhelmed at what this all meant. But I decided then and there that it would not hold him back.

When we received the official written diagnoses, Alex was four. I felt he was old enough to talk about all we had discovered. That afternoon I told Alex that I had just received amazing news and we needed to celebrate. When he asked why, I said it was because the doctor had diagnosed him with ADHD. (I used the same voice I would have used had we won the lottery.) When he asked what that meant, I told him that God had given him more of everything! He had more emotions, energy, talents, physical abilities, and brains. I said he was basically just like Superman. And because he had superpowers there would be lots of challenges. I looked at him very seriously and told him that he had been given a gift (which I believe with my whole heart to be true) and that he would have to work very hard to control it. But that I would be there to help. I also looked up all the famous people that had ADHD, (why hello Michael Jordan and Albert Einstein), and shared with him the other members of the extremely elite club he now belonged to.

When we moved to Texas the summer before his first-grade year, I could not have been more nervous. He barely knew the lower-case alphabet and we were still struggling in so many areas. I had taken him off the medication that the doctor in Connecticut had put him on because he was in a constant state of lethargy and was unable to fall asleep at night. My first attempt at finding a new doctor was a disaster. We went and saw a man named Dr. Lee, who, after a 30-minute appointment, told me that Alex would never function well in society and would eventually be institutionalized. (What the !!!) I wish I were exaggerating. I looked at Dr.

Lee, suggested he be in an institution and walked out. Three doctors later we found an amazing psychologist who believed in parent and child training and gave us lots of tools to work with it. Her encouragement and "homework" helped us make giant leaps forward. Begrudgingly, I agreed to try medication once more after she asked me if I would let him have glasses if he could not see. I told Alex that it would only be temporary until we were able to get some things back on track. I am not sure he slept properly for those two years. He also lost his appetite, so he became a skinny little thing. But it did help calm him and help him focus so we stuck with it for a time.

The new school the boys would attend in Texas was also a Godsend. The principal suggested Alex go back to kindergarten because of his age and his current knowledge level and helped us work through the special education system. I will be eternally indebted to the principal of that school for her kindness and direction during those early years. I am not sure she will ever know the true impact she had on changing a child's trajectory. Teachers, principals, educators—you ABSOLUTELY have the power to change the life of a child. I also chose to befriend each teacher (including his amazing diagnostician) and let them know I would be available if they needed help. (And that I would be watching.) Even as a working single parent, I made sure I was very involved at their school. By the end of his second-grade year he no longer needed to be in special education. After conversations with his teacher (whom we loved as well), I chose to wean him off his Adderall after an insurance change left us having to make some choices. The teacher was on board and knew it could get bumpy, but she was totally supportive. I told Alex he would have these superpowers his entire life, so we needed to begin learning to manage his behavior without medication. (Please know my heart. I am not stating that medication is right or wrong. I know this is not an option for every parent/child. I am just sharing our family's personal story.)

When you spend a lot of time trying to help a child feel valued, it can often come back to bite you. We had a very unexpected development of inflated self-esteem. Alex had spent the first few years of his life believing there was something wrong with him. So, I was bound and determined to convince him that he was amazing. I knew this had been accomplished when in fifth grade his PE teacher (another favorite) sent a note home letting me know that Alex had an unhealthy view of competition. He had told her that it was not his fault that he was beating all the other kids in everything. God had just made him better than everyone else. Well ok then. We might need to work on humility next.

Alex eventually went on to prove crazy Dr. Lee wrong. In junior high, he excelled as an athlete and a student but more importantly he had come to realize that he was made exactly the way God had intended. In high school he lettered in four varsity sports as a freshman, volunteered for multiple organizations, and graduated with honors. In college, Alex was the captain of his football team, an All-American football player, and graduated Magnum Cum Laude. He then went on to get his master's degree in eighteen months. Forgive me for being braggy. Please. But it's as if Every. Single. Line. I type is a victory banner waving at the people and obstacles that tried to hold my child back.

Here's what I'm learning: Sometimes you have to fight even when the people who are supposed to know it all tell you the opposite. This is especially true for moms. You know in your gut when you need to put the gloves on. And put them on we must. There are too many people like Dr. Lee who would like to take the easy road and just relegate these kids to mediocrity, when in fact they were created to move mountains. Listen, I know that some of you are so tired, you feel like you have no fight left. Some days you are lucky just to get out of bed and get them dressed. You feel exhausted, defeated, and unworthy of the task. I wish with all my heart that I could take you by the hands, look you in the eyes, and tell you that you are not alone, and I understand what you are feeling. But you are not done, sister. Far from it. There is more fight in you. More than you will ever know. You just have to find a way to get back to your corner and rest for a bit. Somehow. Some way. And then you will come out swinging again. Because when all is said and done, they are not the only ones you are fighting for.

Last but not least, the baby. And fighting my own insecurities.

ALAN

When Alan was three, he dipped a little girl backwards and kissed her "like Fred Stair," and was removed from Sunday school class. Later he was brought to me because during his turn at Simon Says, he said Simon wanted the class to kiss his butt. He told me afterwards that they just didn't get his joke. He was three. And I was so worried what the teachers thought I was teaching him.

When he was in preschool, he took every single book off the teacher's bookshelf. She was upset. She thought he was being defiant. He thought she was unable to correctly organize her books by color since they were all mixed up. And I got a phone call. When she insisted he place his lunch in the cubby, he slammed the bag on the floor in front of her. Because if she was not going to refrigerate it properly, he wasn't going to eat. I got another phone call. The day he announced that she was unqualified to teach in the words only a four-year-old can muster, she had me come pick him up.

It seemed like Alan was always being "misunderstood." Was I in denial? Did he need more discipline? Spankings? Did I need another parenting book? Or maybe another class? By child number three, my insecurities as a single mom had led to obsessively taking so many classes that I was qualified to teach Systematic Training for Effective Parenting, and I had my own small resource library on parenting. What was even harder was that Alan seemed perfectly ok when he was with me. He was my little buddy I took everywhere, and we had a great time. With almost a seven-year gap between he and his closet brother, it allowed for lots of Mom and Alan time. He occasionally showed some bouts of anger, but as with many things I chalked it up to the lack of having a dad in his life. And, like most single parents I would just overcompensate with extra love. I just wasn't seeing the issues that these teachers were. Was I wrong? Had I finally become THAT parent? Did the teachers think I was a bad parent?!

Just to be safe, before he started kindergarten, I took Alan to the same psychologist that I had taken Alex to in Texas. I just needed some more feedback. The doctor tested him and diagnosed him with ADD. I wasn't one hundred percent sure I agreed with the diagnosis, but I was certain of one thing. He definitely had some superpowers. I just wasn't sure what they were yet. I figured with years of behavioral education in the trenches with his older brother, I was at least somewhat prepared to deal with the challenges that came with Alan's unique abilities. But it turns out I was not even in his league.

When kindergarten rolled around his classroom teacher and his GT teacher seemed to understand his thought process, so that year went much smoother. They shed some light on his extreme intellect and at one point even told me that I may never truly understand his macabre humor or his need to debate because, well basically, I was not on his intellectual level. They said this very kindly, but I had no doubt what they meant. My kid was just wayyyyyyy smarter than me.

In kindergarten just after school started, he came home and said I had to buy a multiplication book because he needed extra help for class. (Wait aren't they just now learning numbers?) Then he had to do a project on his favorite athlete and write a report. He chose Tony Hawk. In first grade, he needed a cursive writing book. Then, he needed a computer program for Spanish. In second grade, he came home and said we needed to go by a tri-fold board because he had to research and do a full report on the president with pictures. (What the heck?) Weren't they still supposed to be learning basic writing? At this point, I'm thinking the teacher is just nuts and we are about to have a serious talk. I went into his class to pick him up one day determined to speak with the teacher. And if you figured it out already, you are quicker than I was. The teacher had no idea what I was talking about. He had been giving himself extra work assignments all this time. Great. I'm parenting Professor X.

Understanding finally dawned on me. He was one of those mythological kids you hear about who actually get bored in school. Wait. They're real? This throws a curve in my stubborn refusal to accept Bigfoot. Knowing Alan needed more, we began a long journey of looking for a school to feed his unusually hungry brain. He went on to an art school, a private school, and a gifted school as he made his way through the elementary years. He continued to "challenge" his teachers, and they continued to "misunderstand" him. And I continued to be worried about what others thought. I could fill a small book with the notes I received. But eventually we all made it out unscarred.

Junior high and high school had its challenges, including a tennis coach that I almost went toe to toe with on a court. But with GT and AP classes, and what I still see as a saving grace: debate, we made it to graduation with our sanity. Alan walked the stage with a stack of honors and the holiest shoes—literal holes—I have ever seen in my life. It was at that moment, seeing those shoes, that I realized at some point along the way I had stopped caring what others thought of me as a parent. And Alan's education was not the only area of his life where I have had to learn to let Alan be Alan. And everyone else's opinion was irrelevant.

Going back to Alan's second birthday, all he wanted was a skateboard like the big kids. I used to joke that when he was born, he was fourteen. In kindergarten, while writing his "self-assigned" report on Tony Hawk, he discovered the origin of skateboards. It's how surfers made it through the cold winters. They added wheels to their boards. He couldn't wait to tell me this because it was obviously the reason he loved skateboarding so much. Since I had moved him from the Outer Banks of North Carolina and he could not surf, skateboarding was the natural progression. By the time he was in first grade, he was a fixture at the local skatepark, and he insisted on dressing like the pros in the magazines. Which meant his clothes always had holes and looked slightly abused. And I owned stock in Vans. There were days when he would make me stand outside the fence surrounding the skatepark because the cursing was so bad, and he didn't want me scolding the teenagers for using potty language around him. Everything about the culture went against what I thought a child should be doing.

There were so many times when I questioned why I was allowing my eight-year-old to hang out somewhere where most of the other kids were high. You have no idea how hard it is to be a helicopter mom hiding in bushes so that your kid can skateboard around possible delinquents. I must have looked ridiculous. I kept it up for years. Seriously. Me, my book, and my bush. It was like a bad country song. When he was 11, he flew alone for the first time to California to skate. I wanted to vomit. His brothers quickly reminded me that they hadn't been allowed to leave the cul-de-sac until they were 16. Allowing Alan to skate, as ridiculous as this sounds, stretched me more as a parent than most other things I can think of. So much of it just felt so unsafe. But I knew early on skateboarding was Alan's love, and I had to let Alan be Alan.

At the time of this writing, Alan is a junior in college, still challenging his professors and still skateboarding. Except now he's the one in the magazines, and I don't have to buy his Vans anymore. They send them to him for free. But more importantly…he is still marching to the beat of his own drum. And I'm still dancing in the background like it's my favorite song.

Here's what I'm learning: I have to let my boys (men) be who they were created to be. And trust them to make the right decisions as they go down the paths that they choose. Even if it's totally different than what I would choose. Even if it scares me. Even if the other moms judge me because of it. In Alan's case, he was born to skateboard and challenge the system. I love that about him. Raising him has opened my eyes to so much, including celebrating people who are absolutely nothing like me. And hopefully one day, I can be as cool as him.

Parenting is exhausting. I mean—phew. Mine are all but grown now and writing all of this has brought back every bit of joy and angst I think I've ever felt raising them. I'm worn out now. And, it doesn't matter if your kids are saints or one step from the pen—it's still hard. Because there is an endless number of villains just waiting to get at them. Such is life. Our job is to equip them with the skills to battle once they leave us. Because when they grow up, the villains grow up too. And the villains are not always so obvious. Insecurities, prejudices, behavioral disorders, the media, false perceptions, childhood trauma, and on and on.... There are countless outside forces waging war against them regardless of what their home environment was like, how much money they had, or how smart they may be. We have to equip them to fight. For themselves. And for others. Especially people who don't look like them. Pray like them. Vote like them. Or love like them. Because we are raising superheroes. And it doesn't matter how old they are—we can never, ever stop fighting for them. Even if it's only on our knees.

CHAPTER 7

HEAVY HEARTS AND CHICKEN LEGS

It's Time to Forgive

"Bitterness is like drinking poison and waiting for the other person to die."

—*Joanna Weaver*

When I was in my twenties, I drank a lot of poison.

I feel I should start this chapter by stating a lot of healing has taken place. And a lot of forgiveness. And my ex-husband and I now have a good relationship. Not a perfect one. I still would like to wop him upside his head occasionally but compared to where we were, it's pretty dang good. (One word: Therapy.) We chat about our kids and grandkids, I invite him to family parties and we occasionally team up when one of the turds needs some redirecting, even though they are all now grown turds. I'm proud of where he is today. In fact, my now husband, Saint Kyle (I'll introduce him soon, he's pretty dreamy), was the one to perform the marriage ceremony for my ex-husband and his new wife, who we call Grandma Kitty. Yes. We are that family.

But, can I just be honest and say for years I secretly wished my ex-husband would be lost in a desert or stranded on an island like Tom Hanks, but never return, and the kids and I would collect his insurance policy? I didn't necessarily wish him harm, I just wanted him to disappear forever. Ok, that's not true. I think one time I wished that he would be mauled by pigmy dinosaurs like in Jurassic Park II.

There was so much hurt I was dealing with from everything we had gone through. There were multiple reasons I was granted full custody of our boys and he only had supervised visitation with law enforcement, and they included violence and substance abuse. On the day of court, he told the judge I was lucky I still had my teeth, so that pretty much put the nail in the custody coffin. After that he all but disappeared for a long time and it was just me and the littles. Who weren't so little anymore.

At the time, my mind was trying to wrap itself around the future. I had spent almost a dozen years trapped in a surreal prison trying to hold everything together so that our boys would have a good life. And it was easier for me to believe somehow it was my fault. That's what unhealthy overachievers do. If something doesn't succeed, we shoulder the blame and work ourselves to the bone to make sure it doesn't happen again. Maybe if I made more money, maybe if I learned to cook better, clean better, if I were skinnier, maybe if I was more successful, maybe if the kids were more successful…maybe, just maybe, he would want to be a good dad. But nothing ever seemed like the magic solution. I could never understand why our amazing kids never seemed reason enough for him to change his life.

I think I could fill a book with my mistakes and past regrets, and why I was no saint. But it took a lot of counseling for me to realize that the kids and I did not deserve his behavior no matter what. And I had to stop blaming myself. And when I stopped shouldering the full weight of his decisions and held him accountable for the years of hell he had put us through, I wasn't suddenly free, I was suddenly angry. And those feelings soon turned into hating him with every ounce of my being. I hated him for what he stole from me and our children. I hated him for the countless affairs. I hated him for the hurt he caused. I hated him for abandoning them. I hated him for all of it!

Until one day I realized I couldn't bear the weight anymore. I did not want a heart of hate. And I didn't want it for my boys either. We needed to forgive him. For all of it. I was learning that unforgiveness is your own personal prison where you are being held captive. And locked alongside you, in that cell, is not only all the pain and bitterness, but the very person you were trying to get away from in the first place. The only way to break free from that jail is through forgiveness.

I hope I am not making this sound easy. Because it is anything but. I spent years battling through hurt and anger and wanting to make someone feel all the pain that I had felt. But keeping a heart full of bitterness was hurting me, not him.

If I could say one thing I would have done differently, it would be that I would have forgiven quicker. If bitterness were measured in physical weight, I think my heart was holding 437 pounds of it. And I have chicken legs y'all. I'm not even sure how I was standing most days. It's hard for your heart to experience the sweetness of gratitude and the bubbles of joy when it's filled to the brim with the hard tar of bitterness. But when you finally decide to release people, when you decide to finally release yourself…that bitterness gets released too. And it's like your heart is so light it could float to the moon.

Forgiving my ex-husband helped heal my heart, but also helped my boys build a stronger relationship with their dad. Which has continued to refine them as men. And through this they too have learned forgiveness and grace. And that you have to love the unhealthy people at a distance sometimes, and often with boundaries, but you still have to love them.

Again, a lot of this is due to Saint Kyle. He told me there was no statute of limitations on being a dad. And that we had to give the boys' dad another chance. It ticked me off at first, because Kyle was supposed to be on my team. And I felt a little betrayed. But because my husband is patient and kind, he helped me see how much the boys would benefit from a healthy dad, and how we should help in any way we can. I eventually saw the wisdom in his words. And I found my heart wanting Mr. Bell to do better also. This was a long journey.

My ex-husband has been sober for many years now. And we have seen many changes. The biggest is with his heart. Although I still think some of his thought processes are dysfunctional and unhealthy, I know his heart is in the right place. And I see how he is doing his best to make up for the times when he wasn't. And my boys do too.

Here's what I'm learning: Forgiveness does not magically rebuild all relationships. Some relationships are toxic and dangerous and need to be avoided. At all costs. But you still need to find a way to forgive. Even if the relationship is not mendable. You need to. For your sake. I know that I am no expert on forgiveness. There is still an old neighbor I think about throat punching for making a racial remark towards one of my kids. That was fifteen years ago. Sometimes you must forgive many times over. It's a journey.

I was helping with a Single Mom Conference a couple years ago and a gentleman named Jay was speaking on forgiveness. He gave four of the most profoundly simple steps to forgiveness I had ever heard:

1. Acknowledge what's been taken from you. Acknowledge what was done to you. Acknowledge what happened. Because none of it is ok. And you did nothing to deserve it.

2. Recognize what cannot be paid back. Because nothing they can do could possibly repay you. Nothing. They cannot give back what was taken.

3. Forgive the debt. Surrender the right to be paid back even when you should be. Then surrender the expectation of justice to God.

4. Know that there may not be reconciliation.

These steps will never make what was done to you ok. But it sure helps to free your heart so that you can make room for the good stuff. Robin Sharma said, "Forgiveness isn't approving what happened. It's choosing to rise above it."

I am finding that the person hardest to forgive is myself. I think of mistakes I made when my kids were little, or poor decisions I made when I was younger and frankly, I feel heartsick. But I know I can never be the person I want to be if I am dragging that baggage. So, I have to pause sometimes and tell myself that the past is the past and I need to look ahead. And I'm learning that forgiveness is something that I have to do often, whether that's my parents, a friend who's hurt me, or even my ex-husband. I must continue to forgive. Every day. Life is way too short to live with a heavy heart and chicken legs.

CHAPTER 8

ANTIQUE GLASS AND ANTIQUE NINJAS

The Thing About Regrets

Y ou know that really cool tattoo that everyone was getting about ten years ago, that says "Regret Nothing"? Yeah, I don't have that tattoo.

I grew up in and around antique stores and flea markets. I don't remember my mom having much of a work history of her own. When she was healthy my dad had her pick out all the surfaces for his construction projects and do the interior decorating. But I think the pressure of that was more than she could bear. I also vaguely remember her running a vintage resale store and working as a florist. I was blessed to witness her floral skills my entire life. But as far as jobs go, nothing seemed to last long. Until she discovered the magic of the flea market. She really really loved her booth at the flea market. And this better fit her emotional capabilities. Because when she couldn't get out of bed, or she needed professional help, or she had the mental capacity of a ten-year-old, or she was zoned out on meds…she didn't have to go to work. And there was no one to fire her. And when she was at her best, she was able to do what seemed to make her most happy: collect old things. She would hit garage sales and thrift stores, estate sales and other flea markets to build up her inventory. And she was good. She found treasures that people were selling for next to nothing. She was kind of a hoarder now that I stop to really think about it.

By the time I was twelve, I knew the difference between milk glass, carnival glass, depression glass, and mercury glass. And to this day I can still spot a piece of McCoy pottery a mile away. Mama eventually fell away from the flea markets as well. Because on top of her other troubles, she was also a severe hypochondriac. So even her imaginary illnesses kept her in bed. As she became more dependent on medications and sank deeper into her mental illnesses, her beloved antiques and green thumb were no longer strong enough to keep her present in reality.

By the time I was nineteen and headed to Hawaii, she was becoming more and more of a ghost, and the glimpses of who she was grew further and further apart. And I was mad. Really mad. Mad at her for abandoning me during my childhood. Mad at her for letting me go to school dirty. Mad at her for not teaching me that I was worth something and that boys couldn't fix me. Mad at her for not fighting for her life. Mad at her for not fighting for mine. Mad at her for not being there for my little brother. Mad at her for being weak. And eventually, I began to treat her exactly like my dad had. With a measure of impatience, apathy, and worst of all, disgust. Sadly, during the following two decades, my scars hardened into unbreakable chains that guarded my heart. Because I equated her lack of fighting for her life to her lack of love for me. If she loved us, why didn't she do whatever she could to get better?

It's important to pause, for me to share that it was not just my mom that had a love of medications. It was most of my family. I was raised surrounded by the belief that medications fix everything. They truly believed this. Whatever ails you can be fixed with a magical pill. It was like an extremely demented version of Allison in Wonderland. "Eat this. Drink that." And so, everyone in my family became medicated. And then everyone became addicted. (Squirrel: I was blessed to be extremely allergic to multiple medications and terrified of the rest. So, for all my friends who wonder why I won't even take aspirin…now ya know.)

When I would go home to visit during the next fifteen years, my mom's decline continued. I would try to prepare myself mentally to not get upset or react to her condition, and that would last for about 24 hours. But by day 2, the hurts seemed to bubble up and her medicated prison infuriated me. By this time, my dad was not far behind her. His dependency on pills rivaled hers. I knew my parents were both getting less and less able to exist on their own, and I had no idea how they were surviving. So, once I became financially stable, I tried on multiple occasions to convince them to move from Virginia to Texas so that I could better help. But no one leaves the coast in my family. No one except me.

Eventually, my visits home became fewer and fewer. It was hard to watch what I perceived as their chosen decline, and I didn't want my boys around the dysfunction. I worked so hard to break free from that life and I knew I was never going to subject them to it. Finally. it got to the point where I only went home once a year. Or for funerals. And those came quickly. And often.

My dad had severe arthritis in his neck and sacroiliac joints, both sides. And he had multiple spinal fusions. The pain he powered through in his youth was now just constantly numbed by pills. And a lifetime of over-medication eventually took its toll on his body. My dad smoked as well. So, between the cigarettes and the pills, eventually his body gave up. I dreaded going home for the funeral, because I wasn't sure how my mom would act. Suffice it to say she missed the funeral because she decided to make a large cocktail of pills and ended up in the hospital getting her stomach pumped.

At the time, I had an older sister, Lori, and younger brother, Joshua, living in Virginia. And one older sister, Wendy, living in North Carolina.

Our extended family was scattered between the two, Virginia and Carolina. I was in Texas. I offered to bring Mom back to Texas with me because she basically needed someone to watch her full time. All my siblings thought that was a bad idea. (My relationships with my siblings were never the same after I left home.) So, they decided Lori and Joshua would take over care of my mom. When I voiced concerns because they both had their own battles, I was told to pack my things and carry my snotty ass back to Texas.

My oldest sister Lori was born with a disease in her hips, which was made worse by a car accident as a teenager. Lori had the kindest soul. She was the person who would give you the shirt off her back. I always thought of her as a purple butterfly. I'm not sure why. My little brother Joshua was handsome and smart and talented, and never believed he was good enough for anything. But he was my childhood buddy. And we chased trains, stole collards from our neighbor, and tried to catch bats during the summers in a crab net. And like the rest of my family, both were extremely addicted to prescription meds. These were the self-appointed care givers for my mama.

Shortly after my dad died, my younger brother mixed a variety of street pills and overdosed. He was at my sister's, "helping" to take care of my mom. My mom was the one who found him. She was barely recovering from the loss of my dad. We all were. I am not sure how she made it through my little brother's funeral.

Less than a year later, my sister Lori, who was taking care of my mom, also died. Pills and street drugs. And I headed home to plan a third funeral. And again, I don't know how my mom made it through. How do you lose your spouse, and then your son, and daughter, and not die of heartache?

The only sibling left, my sister Wendy, was still in her own battle with pills, so after the funeral I rented a suburban, and loaded up my mom for a very long drive to Texas. (Side note: Wendy has been clean for many years now and is doing amazing. And I thank God every day for her.)

I need to add that the things I did that made my siblings build a wall to keep me out after I left home, were the same things I thought would bring us closer. I figured if they saw that I was able to get out and be successful, it would show them they had a chance also. But with each accomplishment they just clasped their hands tighter and fortified the stronghold that kept me out. It was like the childhood game we played at school. Red Rover Red Rover. But no matter how hard and fast I ran I could not break apart the chain they had created. And I never made it through. They just kept sending me back to the other side. So, I buried my siblings without them truly knowing how much I love them. And I miss them so much it hurts.

The drive back to Texas with my mom was long and confusing. I was still in shock. Mostly because I hadn't processed the first two funerals, much less a third. And now I was a single parent of three boys and the caregiver of a mom who spoke in monosyllabic sentences.

I thought going through a divorce and single parenting was hard—until I brought my mentally ill, overly-medicated mother back to Texas. Holy Hannah. Those were some hard, dark days. And it was equally hard on the boys. Not only was their normally rock-solid mom acting like a bit of a nutter, but their grandmother was going through hallucinogenic periods while we were adjusting her medications. She would quietly walk in their rooms and it would scare the crap out of them. And she would talk to people who weren't there. It is still one of the hardest things I ever went through. My mama went by Nina, because when we were little, my cousin wasn't able to pronounce Linda, so she called her Aunt (pronounced aint) Nina. It stuck. So, to all the nieces and nephews and grandkids she was Nina. When I would text my boys anything about "Nina," autocorrect would change it to "Ninja." And because of her habit of sneaking into places without you knowing it, we adapted it as her new name.

Once mom was in our home, I kicked into overachiever-drill-sergeant-fixit mode, probably not the healthiest choice but… After a year of doctors, therapists, and lifestyle changes, my mom went from a dozen plus medications to four. And a person appeared that I didn't know was there. She was able to hold actual conversations. And she became a real human again. And I discovered although there was a lot of damage, there was a lot of person left still.

She eventually got well enough that for the first time in her life she was able to live on her own and mostly care for herself. I was very proud, and so was she. She had a tiny apartment with lots of plants and seashells and a bird she named Sammie. She still needed a lot of help but she was pretty independent too. Sadly, most of the feelings that I carried over from childhood still dictated my actions. I still kept her at an arm's length. I was still mostly impatient. And I was still not able to show her the love that she needed. I basically treated her like a child I was tasked to take care of. I was never mean, but I was never as loving as I should have been. I guess I treated her with a mixture of firmness, kindness, and disconnect. I had forgiven her for the hurt she caused me, but I never took the time to learn to love her. And I wish I could do it all over again. She had lost everyone. What she needed was love from her daughter. It's still gut wrenching to think about, and I regret every moment.

Because my mom smoked and also wore her body down from countless medications, after less than two years in her tiny home, she was hospitalized multiple times for heart issues. For a while she managed to recover each time and was able to go home. But the last time she was hospitalized they said she would not recover. So, we called in hospice. And that's when all the emotions came crashing in. And for the first time in my life, I was not mad at her. She was no longer the drug addict, or the woman who neglected me when I was little, and abandoned me when I was teenager. She was just my mom. The mom who made things pretty. The mom who loved to watch American Pickers with me. The mom who grew the most beautiful gardens. The mom who collected antique glass. The mom who loved every single person she met. And for the first time I had no trouble actually loving her. Why had I not been strong enough to do it earlier?

My mom was in the hospital with hospice for almost a month. And either my husband or I were with her every moment. Some nights we both slept there. So, I could listen to her breathe. My best friend Prissy came up often as well. At first, my mom was able to talk some. One day while we were watching American Pickers and I was giving her small sips of protein drink, she said softly, "Hey Bird, remember that time we went to the movies…that was fun." I smiled and said yes mama and walked straight outside and cried so hard I thought my chest would burst. Because that was the only time I had taken her to a movie. One freaking time. And it is still one of the greatest regrets I have. Was I so busy with my "important life," or so mad at her from 25 years earlier that I couldn't find time for something so small? She didn't talk much longer. And eventually she closed her eyes and we held her hand for almost two weeks longer. Her little heart just kept beating. There was nothing left of her, but she just wouldn't let go. And neither would I. It was like I had waited my whole life for a mama, and now she was here and I didn't want our time together to end.

One night, the evening before Father's Day, a hospice nurse gave me some advice. I'm not sure if you have ever spent much time at a hospital but when you are up there for close to a month, the nurses become like family. And hospice nurses are a special breed of angels. She told me I had to tell my mom it was time to go. Because she was holding on. But I was holding on too. I wanted every second I could get with her. That night before I went to sleep, I hugged her and told her that she needed to go be with my dad. And my siblings. I told her the next day was Father's Day and it would make dad so happy for her to come home. I let her know we would all be ok. It was time. I had spent 27 previous nights being awoken by beeping sounds and nurses. But that night I slept the entire night. When I awoke, it was almost 7:00 am. I hopped up panicked, but she was still there, heart beating away. I walked over to say good morning and noticed a slight difference in her breathing. I pointed it out to the nurse who was standing there but she said everything looked the same. As did the nurse changing her drip line. That's when I quietly said I thought she was getting ready to leave, and asked them would the give us privacy. They looked at me like I was crazy, but immediately left. I held my mom's hand and prayed with her, I called my sister and put her on speaker. I played one of my mom's favorite songs. And as my sister and I said goodbye and told her to go, she took her last breath.

That time with my mom was a gift. My husband, Saint Kyle, says it was one of the sweetest times in his life. And I cherished every second. But I still wish to this day I would have done things differently. I hear people often say that they regret nothing. I do. I regret not loving my mama sooner.

There was not a lot of beauty in my mama's life. And what there was I cling to almost desperately. I love all things floral and can see her in every wildflower field. I collect milk glass, and keep my eyes out for rare finds. It's almost like by loving the things she loved so much, I am loving her as well. I can't count how many times I have just sat and cried, and told her I was sorry for not coming to get her sooner. But then I get to take solace in the fact that the only thing she loved more than flowers, and gardening, and antiques, was her Jesus. And I have no doubt that she is overflowing with peace and joy as she sits at His feet among the wildflowers.

Here's what I'm learning: Emotions are good. They are necessary. But they can also get in the way. They can cause you to miss out. There are some emotions that need to be let go of to make room for the good ones. I am learning to listen to my emotions with my heart but filter them through my head. We have a heart *and* a mind. Our emotions are there to help guide the train. Not drive the train.

If you asked my mom if she was good at anything, she'd say no. But she could grow anything. And vintage goods weren't all she collected. She also collected people. The ones who no one else had time for. The ones others called weird, or unwanted. The different ones. My mom loved everyone. And everyone had a place at her table. And when you leave space at your table for the people who may not be welcome other places, you are changing two lives.

That's the lesson I want to take from her life. Love everybody. Always.

CHAPTER 9

SALTY LANGUAGE AND HANDSOME CLERGYMEN

Tearing Down the Walls

"You are confined only by the walls you build yourself."
—Andrew Murphy

I grew up in a construction family. Like generations of builders. I have personally been in the building industry for well over two decades. I tell people I am far more construction worker than I am designer. I also spent my first 20 years on the coast, so I have grown up around fishermen. Ever heard of the phrases "Mouth of a sailor," or "Construction Language?" Well, I grew up deeply immersed in both. So basically, it's not my fault that I have a potty mouth—I was born with salt in it. Could be my worst rationalization ever. But there it is. The good news, I had a very proper grandmother who trained me well, so I keep a controlled tongue in most environments. Public speaking, podcasts, working with small children, etc. However, in times of shock or nervousness…well…it's never pretty.

In September of 2007, my sweet friend Angie invited me to a concert benefitting our local education foundation. The evening of, I ended up working late and I was just too tired to go. I called to let her know. She proceeded to tell me she was going to stand in front of the stadium and wait for me and if I didn't show up, she was probably going to be kidnapped. (She's dramatic also.) So I caved. I was late arriving, so once she met me downstairs, she told me there were already quite a few people in the reserved suite. Including, in her words, a good-looking metrosexual who I could talk to because he wasn't her type (she loves cowboys). However, she knew good and well I was not looking to talk to anyone. Period. She was also a single mom and she knew my heart on the matter. And my heart was set.

Looking back…if I'm being honest, I think some bitterness had settled in my heart toward all men. After Mr. Bell left for good, I had gone on an occasional date but I absolutely was not looking for a relationship. As time passed, I think I just built up a wall of resentment toward the male species as a whole. Also, I had made a promise to myself that I would not bring men around my boys. Another decision I had made was not marrying until they were out of the house. Because if any of these boys had a nightmare or a bad night and they needed their mom, that space would be open. If you're a boy mom, you know they don't often want to snuggle their mom. So, I could not picture them wanting to crawl up on the bed in their snuggly pj's if a new stepdad was there. I was also insanely protective of my boys. To a fault, I admit. But they had already been through enough and single parenting is difficult as it is. So, a boyfriend was just not an option for me. And after some time, I think I became so jaded I didn't even want friends who were male. I was mad at them all.

As I took my seat that night, I agreed with Angie's description. There was a good-looking gentleman dressed very dapper in the suite. Which ticked me off. I'm not sure why. And then he spoke to me. Oh, bless him. Did he not see the bitterness radiating off of me like a toxic waste can at a nuclear plant? I should have been wearing one of those signs around my neck like you see on the back of biohazard trucks that warn people not to get to close. He said hello. I made a rude grunt. He asked where I was from, I told him and did not ask where he was from but he told me anyway. South Florida. He asked did I like hockey, I replied, "Hockey is stupid." And so on. He seemed unaffected by my curt nature. Very good looking. Bad social register.

Finally, the concert was over. I hugged Angie and raced for the exit. Mr. Metro had left a few minutes earlier, so I made my escape. As I got closer to my car, he had the audacity to pull up and try to talk to me. What is it with this guy! So, I got my speech ready. The one I had given so many times before. The one that just wacked them upside their heads and sent them running for the hills. My self-righteousness was like a second skin now. He rolled down his window and said, "Hi. I was wondering since you missed most of the concert if you would like to attend another with me for a different fundraiser next week?" And then I let him have it. "First of all, I don't date. I am a very very busy working mother running not one, but two businesses and I am a single parent of three boys on top of that. And they are very busy with their athletics and academics. They take up all my time, and I am not looking for a relationship. Because if they ever want to hop in my bed on a stormy night there does not need to be a weird man in my bed. Do you understand?" (Yes. I said all of this to a perfect stranger. But wait. It gets worse.) As I was now bleeding my self-righteousness I added, "Also, I am very involved in my church. And…I love Jesus." After this, I expected him to run for the hills. But that's not what happened. He smiled and said, "Wow, that's so interesting. I'm a pastor." Was this man making fun of me? I cocked my head and said, "Bull$#!t." (Enter the salty language I warned you of.) He reached over and pulled out a Bible that was sitting on his seat. On the cover embossed in gold read "Reverend Kyle Rodgers." Holy $#!t. I vaguely remember feeling sweaty and muttering a series of unintelligible remarks. He smiled again and calmly said, "So, what about the concert?" And the rest, my friends, is history.

I could write and entire book on the journey of me and Saint Kyle. It would include the fact that he dated me for seven years before we married because he knew how important it was for me to raise my boys. He also knew we both had walls that needed taken down. (Side Note—it was my boys who finally insisted we go ahead and get married so that I would quit being a helicopter parent and have someone else to focus my attention on. Ungrateful little turds.) I would also include how good he was to my boys. I would tell about how we knew that we would be together forever by the third date. And an entire chapter would be about how, even during our trials and struggles, I knew without a doubt that he was pure gold. He is kindness embodied. He loves all people. And if you have a rocky past, then he is your guy. Because he doesn't love the perfect people. He loves the messy people. He loves the real, authentic, salt of the earth people.

But…I almost missed out.

When you are hurt, you build up walls to protect yourself. And remember, I'm in construction. So I build strong walls. Some walls keep bad stuff out. I like to call those walls boundaries. They are good to have. They keep you safe. Healthy. But those are not the ones I'm talking about. I'm talking about the ones that keep good stuff out. Those are bad walls. Mine were mostly the latter. They were built of strong bricks made from a mixture of bitterness, over-achievement, sarcasm, constant work, and self-righteousness. And they were placed there not just for fear of getting hurt again, but for fear of allowing someone to discover I was not good enough. That's what you do when you're broken. And I was afraid that if someone saw I was just a pile of shards then they would realize I wasn't worth anything. But Kyle is tall and strong and patient. So, he didn't mind peering over the walls while I was slowly dismantling them. And there were definitely times that I took one brick down and put two back up.

(Squirrel: And we must chase this one, it's too good. Kyle comes from a background totally different than mine. His parents were married until his dad passed away, and they only take Tylenol. They are all happy and encouraging and they do not have potty mouths. So, I was terrified to meet them. My prayer was to make it through the meal without saying a bad word. I was so nervous I could barely speak. I tried to make small talk, but it ended in absolute disaster. His mom mentioned she sometimes thought about getting a puppy. She was in her seventies and she said she was not sure she had the energy. So, I suggested she get a fat dog. [What does that even mean?] Then she mentioned that she would have to take it out to go potty and she didn't like the idea of cleaning up the poop. Do you know what I said?! I responded with, "You could teach him to eat it." [Ohmygosh what?!] I began to feel faint. What the hell did I just say.)

My sweet Saint Kyle also had walls too. His were not so tall, but just as strong, and I too had to be patient. After 20 plus years of marriage Kyle's wife had begun to act increasingly unstable. She was erratic and unpredictable. She threatened separation. She threatened the other staff at the church Kyle worked at. She threatened Kyle. There were rumors of her infidelity but nothing concrete. Things continue to spiral—Kyle left his position at the church. His wife left him. For the orthodontist. Who she had been seeing for almost two years. Kyle was devasted. He lost everything important to him in one fell swoop. His ex-wife took one son and Kyle took the other. The divide was devastating for all. When I met Kyle, he was still dealing with lots of confusion and rejection. At the time he was working for a sports team and trying to find his place in this world. Then he moved on to run an oil company and his spirit seemed to fade. But, one of my favorite parts of our story is watching the walls he built come tumbling down as he went back to what he was designed, called, and gifted to do. I thank God every day that I was allowed to be a small part of his journey back home to leadership. Because his best work is loving people well.

The amazing part about tearing down walls is that it opens the way for the good stuff. Kyle is not just my husband. He is my person. My best friend. My adventure buddy. My exercise pal. My furniture-building, cat-loving, best-spiked-eggnog-making, ex-football-playing, hunk of burning love. And I'm just so thankful that I didn't miss out on the person who listened out for my mama as she slept, and held me as I cried myself to sleep. I believe with my whole heart that everyone deserves a Kyle. Or. . . at least a Saint by another name.

Here's what I'm learning: walls come in all shapes and sizes, and some can be deceptively simple. Sarcasm, work, perfectionism, comparison, fear. These are all walls I have built. But I am taking steps to dismantle them. And figuring out what they are was the first step.

What walls have you built? What makes you shut down? What do you use to keep others out? What touches something in you that causes you to spiral or explode? This is a good place to begin. Start by just letting one person in. Someone who has proven themselves trustworthy. I've found that when I let someone in, I feel more like myself. And go slow. Your walls don't need to all come down at once like Jericho 2.0. Take your time. But take that first step.

There is so much beauty and adventure waiting for us in this world. It's right there. Do you see it? Just past that wall.

CHAPTER 10

MISTAKEN IDENTITY AND HANDY HUSBANDS

The danger of assumptions.

"Making assumptions simply means believing things are a certain way with little to no evidence that shows you are correct, and you can see at once how this can lead to terrible terrible trouble."

—*Lemony Snicket*

I was once working on a design job and I needed to pick up a couple of pillows from my upholsterer. The part of town where his shop is located has a few store fronts with bars on the windows and there is the occasional number painted on the brick to call for a good time. Mine's not up there. Now, I'm quite sure it is a perfectly safe area, I have been there many many times without incident, but the bars do tend to create an unsettling affect on me. I get a bit jumpy. Just being honest. These pillows I was picking up were leather on the back, and the fronts were made from the pelt of an elk. And they were freaking heavy. (Hang in there, this is an important detail.) I left the shop and walked around to the passenger side of my car to put the pillows on the front seat. I opened the door, and Holy

Hannah, my heart stopped. There was a very large man covered in hair, sitting in the driver's seat of my car. I screamed at the top of my lungs and threw the 20-pound pillows as hard as I could at his face, then spun around and ran like hell. I turned to look to make sure he was not following me and as I looked, I noticed there were two... black...Lincoln...MKXs. Uh huh. And then the lightbulb went off. That wasn't my car. My walk of shame back was no joke y'all. As I walked passing the first black car (my car) and the empty space between, I saw the man still sitting in his vehicle with the passenger door open, looking totally shocked. Because let's face it, he was just attacked. Some crazy blonde woman opened his car door, screamed at him, and then threw brick pillows at his face and ran off. Bless his heart. So, I timidly reached for my pillows and in a loud whisper begged, "oh my gosh I'm so sorry." He just stared at me slack jawed. I slowly backed away, got in MY car, and left.

Sadly, this is by no means the only time I have done something like this. There seems to be a corner of my brain that likes to quickly come to conclusions on any number of given subjects. This can relate to people, places, or things. I don't know what triggers it, and I don't like it. So I am trying actively to be aware of when I am making assumptions and may need to dig a little deeper before assuming anything. This requires slowing down, asking questions, and processing. Which is sooooo hard for my personality. I once had a friend tell me that I show up to the saloon with my guns drawn before I even know there is a fight. I'm still not great at it but I'm working on it. Because you know what they say about people who assume...

Just a little more investigation would have helped me out so much on so many occasions. I am learning that being patient and asking a few questions is great preventative medicine to the wrong assumption virus.

About a year after Kyle and I started dating, I realized he was not what you would call "handy." Tall...kind...handsome? Yes. Could he cook? Oh yeah. Handy? Not so much. He had offered to help me change out my front door handle. Yes, it was something I could have done myself, but it was so nice having someone willing to help. After a couple of hours of sweat and kindergarten expletives, (Kyle does not share my potty mouth at all) the task was mostly completed, and he seemed exhausted. So, I decided it would be best to preserve his self-esteem by handling any repairs or improvements from that point on. Shortly after our marriage he went to shut off a valve to a hot water heater that was leaking, and the entire house filled with gas and we all had to evacuate—furthering my beliefs that his handyman skills were all but missing.

Two years into our marriage we bought our first home together, and it was definitely a fixer upper. Located on lots of land with barns and stables, it was what we had been praying for. But the inside needed lots of love. The first time we walked through, my eyeballs burned. On top of removing and adding walls, all the surfaces needed updating and or replacing. Since we were going to have a very limited budget to make said changes, we would be doing a lot of the labor ourselves. I allotted a certain amount of money to hire one of the sub-contractors I had been working with for years to come do the "skilled" work...laying tile, wood, moldings, etc., and then we would do as much as we could to help. I was concerned we had not set enough money aside to pay him for everything on our list. My sweet husband thought it could speed up the process and stretch our dollars if he assisted in everything. Ruh-roh Shaggy. I immediately had visions of missing digits and crooked joints. Mentally, I patted him on the head and thought, aww that's cute, but no thank you. I asked him had he ever laid flooring or hung trim before. To which he replied "yes." And in a somewhat disbelieving tone I replied, "really...when?" He said, "a few different places actually." Then he proceeded to tell me he used to own a ton of tools. I'm sorry, what?! My train was being derailed y'all. It turns out this man that I have now been with almost a decade had in fact not only laid flooring on multiple occasions, he had also painted, done some woodworking, tiling, and trim work, and so on, and so forth. And I'm sorry, how did I NOT know this?!

Turns out there was a lot I did not know about my husband's skills. Sadly, I had never asked. He worked alongside Eliut (our GC) through our entire renovation, and what he didn't know, Eliut taught him, and he executed like a boss. On top of that he also gave me fabulous beaded board ceilings, hung an antique barn door I had salvaged from an old farm for my pantry, designed an amazing reclaimed wood wall, and built me beautiful open shelving in my kitchen. All those years I was under the assumption that my husband was not handy. Not only is he handy, but he's gifted and finds so much joy in it. Ya think ya know a guy.

After living in our precious house for more than a year, I was struggling to find a square farmhouse table that would seat 10 to 12. We have a big family, so we needed a big table. Everything I found was either too small or the wrong look. Then it dawned on me…I'll design a table and Kyle can build it for me. Even just typing those words creates a well of emotions in me. If you would have told me a few years prior that my husband would be building a table for our home, I would have said you were sweet, but just a little coo coo for cocoa puffs. Because I had made the very wrong assumption that my husband was not handy. How many years had I limited him because I had assumed, he couldn't do something? And how much had I missed out on? That experience was a paradigm shift.

Here's what I'm learning: It's easy for me to limit myself and others with false assumptions. This was a pill I desperately needed to swallow. Because it can also cause unnecessary hurt and confusion. I never ever want to deliberately hurt someone's heart or miss out on something or someone beautiful because I was too quick to come up with the wrong conclusion. This is especially important when meeting people who are nothing like me. How different would our world look if we stop making unnecessary assumptions and judgements of others before we get to know them?

So, here's my new practice. It's simple. Slow down. Ask questions. Lots of questions. This is the antidote to assumptions. It's amazing how much you learn when you take the time to gain knowledge and perspective. And remember what your third-grade teacher said: there's no such thing as a dumb question.

CHAPTER 11

SHOWER CURTAINS AND HARRY POTTER

Own your Strengths and Weaknesses

"Owning your weaknesses does not diminish your strengths: it shows your courage."

—Erin Andrews

I think babies smell. There. I said it. And when they first come out, they sort of gag me. Especially when that little black thing is still attached to their naval. Oy vey. I almost threw up just typing that. I pretty much would prefer not to hold one until they are four. Not months. Years. Ok, I'm mostly kidding but not really. I know I know, how did I raise my own children? Not sure. But I think I blocked some parts out. Basically, I am one of the few people on this planet who does not like babies. (And I'm slightly afraid of them.) I love baby showers if the baby is not present. I know I'm horrible. I have grandchildren now, and I have improved. A bit. I'd prefer not to hold them till their little head stops flopping around like a catfish, and that spot on their skull firms up. I do make one exception though. If you wrap them up super tight like a burrito, and place them on my lap, surrounded by blankets and walled in with pillows, I will read to them until the cows come home. That is my jam. Give me a child of any size and a good book and I am in my element.

When my boys were little, I coveted those moments. The times when we were able to forget all the hard stuff going on in our life and just get lost in the words of Dr. Seuss or any number of other authors. I read to them every day and they are still some of my most precious memories. The smell of libraries still creates a euphoria in me like no other.

(Squirrel: One-time Alex almost killed me while I was reading. I was laying on the floor, up against our fireplace in our "little single mom" house, reading *Harry Potter and the Goblet of Fire* to all three of the boys. When I read, Alex liked to walk back and forth up on the hearth that ran the length of our living room. On one of his passes he knocked over the set of wrought iron fireplace tools onto my head. My next memory is hearing Alan wail, "you killed mom," and Alex crying. Andy was busy deciding who to call. I was only knocked out momentarily, and there was no real harm done. But the poker had busted my nose, so the sight of blood only added to the drama. I'm not sure anyone was permanently scarred that day, but Alex has been unusually agreeable ever since.)

Being a single mom of three incredibly busy little boys was my greatest schooling on the power of owning your weaknesses *and* strengths. Because there is no way to hide under the magnifying lens that is parenting. There were just some things I was not going to be very good at. Period. (Including hunting and throwing Spanish daggers.) I refer to them as "squishy skills" and "improvement areas." We all have them. And we all have differing opinions on which of these are important. For instance, I have always wanted a steel stomach. But that's totally not what I have. It's weak. Really-really weak. I take squeamish to another level. I am basically a semi-professional "retcher." If it were an Olympic sport, I would be on a freaking cereal box. But it made being a boy mom extra challenging. Think about it. Almost everything about boys is gross. Things they do, how they smell, what they eat... (Squirrel: One time I threw up in my lap in front of Andy's Junior High School because he placed a frog eye in my palm that he had heisted from his science class.)

Another area that I had to continually work on was my propensity to be an insufferable helicopter mom. This was one of my squishiest skills. Picture a blonde ponytail acting as a propeller and my big mouth making whoosh—whoosh—whoosh noises. Coaches especially loved to see me coming in for a landing.

My worst helicopter catastrophe was when Alan was three and he decided he was brave enough to graduate from taking a bath to taking a shower. Well I was so excited I just *had* to peek. So, while he was in the shower I stood up on the toilet and peeked over the shower curtain while holding onto the rod. All was good until the toilet lid slipped sideways, the curtain rod came loose, and I fell forward, trapping his tiny wet body underneath the shower curtain. Needless to say, he did not shower again for a very long time.

I knew my hovering was an issue, so I tried to keep myself grounded but it was a challenge. My boys will tell you I still struggle with it to this day. But I'm working on it. That's part of owning your weaknesses, right? Recognizing where you need to improve and then working on it. And there are so so many areas I need to improve in. But we must be careful that we are not obsessing over those things. I think that can be a tendency for lots of us—to concentrate hard on things we need to improve on and miss all our amazing strengths.

I don't know about you, but I can be my own worst critic. However, I find that concentrating on what I'm good at is way more gratifying and productive. Acknowledge the things you are good at, then build upon them. And if you have been beat down for so long that you feel you can't seem to find any strengths right now, ask someone you trust to help you identify some things you are good at. You may be shocked by the gifts they see in you. It's amazing what an outside perspective brings to the table. This applies to noticing the strengths of others as well. If you have the opportunity to catch someone doing something well and praise them, you have the opportunity to change their trajectory forever.

There were times when I would lay my head down at night, exhausted, covered up with feelings that I just didn't have enough "strengths" to raise these little boys on my own. It was those times I had to remind myself of what I knew to be true regardless of what I was feeling. And I knew there were some things I was good at. Like making a mean breakfast, or being able to wrestle for hours, or having the patience to read 197 bedtime stories. And I was pretty good at teaching kindness and generosity even what we didn't have two nickels to rub together. And maybe I didn't know anything about weapons (which my boys loved), but I could certainly buy tickets to a gun show and dress us all like cowboys and plan a historically based dinner of frontier food, like the super nerd that I am. Could I help with math? Heck no! Did we almost go to state with our science projects? Yes! Don't even get me started on the art of Valentine's mailboxes. And do my boys remember whether I knew the names of specific cars, or sporting positions? Absolutely not. But do they remember the time I dressed them all in pink sweatshirts at Disney World and harbor a bit of resentment because of it? Yes! Wait. That's not where I was going with that. But you catch my drift.

Here's what I'm learning: Whatever situations we find ourselves in it's important to own our strengths and weaknesses. But building on our strengths is key. That's how we succeed. We all need to take some time to really dig and develop things we are good at and things that bring us joy. When we recognize our strengths, we grow in who we were meant to become. Often the weaknesses not only work themselves out—they also don't have as much power over us. My hovering nature, weak stomach, and propensity to want to bond over the color pink may not have been my greatest assets as a boy mom. But I didn't let them hold me back from being the best mom I could possibly be either. I just owned them and moved on. And let my strengths do the talking. I think it's far more rewarding for all of us.

CHAPTER 12

WEEDS AND WILDFLOWERS

Perspective Changes Everything

"What you see and what you hear depends a great deal on where you are standing. It also depends on what sort of person you are."

—*CS Lewis*

Shortly after moving to Texas with my children from Coastal Carolina, we were almost swept up in a tornado while driving down I-20. Imagine heading down the highway, you're belting out the lyrics to Pat Benatar's "Love is a Battlefield," and suddenly, a tornado touches down right in front of you! I literally had to swerve off the road to avoid ending up in Oz. Then as quickly as it touched down it disappeared. Poof. No trace of the twister. Now, completely shaken, I hear a siren behind me, and I'm being pulled over by a state trooper. My heart was racing, the children were crying, and the cat was flying around the inside of the vehicle like a ping pong ball making awful hissing noises. Wait. Why was there a cat in our vehicle? No. I need to stay on track. Anyways…I assumed the officer was checking on us and I was about to receive some much-needed sympathy…and possibly a pat on the back for my courageous driving maneuvers. The officer asked if we were alright. To which I replied, "not really." I'm sure I must have had crazy eyes and heavy breathing. Then he mentioned my out of town plates, and asked where I was headed. At this point I don't understand why he's being so calm in the presence of a NATURAL DISATER. And then he had the nerve to ask why I was driving erratically. Erratically? ERRATICALLY? Dumbfounded, I replied (possibly with a tinge of snark), that I was obviously outrunning the tornado. He looked at me with his mouth gaping open like I had lettuce growing out of my ears. Then with an equally snarky tone, he announced that there was no tornado, that it was a Dust Devil. Now I looked at him like he had lettuce ears. When I asked what a Dust Devil was, he proceeded to give me an unnaturally loud lecture about weather in West Texas, the wheelbase on my vehicle, and warnings about my driving. Then he just walked away. Just like that. Sauntered back to his vehicle. So, I got out and threw my flip flop at the back of his head. No, I didn't. I'm totally kidding. But I thought about it.

If perspective were a mirror, mine would be like one of those giant carnival mirrors that distorts everything to ridiculous proportions. To that trooper it was a Dust Devil. To me it was certain death. I can be dramatic like that. And I often allow my perspective to get in my own way. It's one of the things I'm working on. I think the wrong perspective can make you miss out on some of the good stuff in life. But keeping your mind open, especially to how others see things, can open a whole world of possibilities.

When I was a little girl I would sit outside on our front porch and watch my mama tend her gardens. She was always at peace outside. I think her gardens were her happy place. Mine too. I can still remember the wonderful smells that marked my childhood. We had honeysuckles growing on every surface that didn't move. And she could grow anything. She had more varieties of flowers than I could wrap my tiny brain around. She had rose bushes, daisies, irises and wild flowers as far as you could see. I liked to ask her the names of all the different flowers. "What's that one called mama?" Over and over and over. And I don't ever remember her tiring of answering. She just repeated the names patiently. And whenever I asked if something was a wildflower or a weed, she always gave the same reply, "They're whatever you want them to be."

And you know what? I want them to be wildflowers…all of them.

With my whole heart, I want to be the sort of person who sees beauty and possibilities and adventure everywhere. I want to be positive and kind always. But I think my somewhat rocky start in life tends to make me more cautious and skeptical at times. And negative if I'm not on constant alert. A life that has had abuse or neglect can cause that. So I have to be ready to remind myself to have the best possible perspective that I can with people and situations. Again, this is not always easy. But it is always worth it. For the past couple of years, I have had a quote in my office that has helped me with this. Its origin is debated, and I have seen several different versions, but the one I love goes like this, "Anyone can find the dirt—be the one that finds the gold." I use it as a mantra of sorts. Especially in times when I don't know what to feel, or negativity would be easier.

Have you ever met someone who is off-putting right from the get-go? It's almost like they decided not to like you before they even met you. This is the perfect example of when I will quietly recite the quote in my head. "Find the gold." And I smile and I make the conscious decision to be kind and hunt for gold. And almost always I end up breaking down whatever wall they had, and a new friendship is made. Will there be those people who this doesn't work with? Absolutely. But hey, that's their loss.

Here's what I'm learning: Life is so much better when you check your perspective. I have to be on constant alert to see things from the best perspective I can. Especially when I'm not sure how I feel. I try and see things how others see them. When I can understand a situation from someone else's point of view it can create understating on levels I never imagined. Simple questions can help change my perspective also. And create healing I could never imagine as well. I am also learning that having a positive perspective is a daily practice. It's not easy. But it helps create appreciation and gratitude in even the heaviest of circumstances. And that is where joy blooms. Ultimately how we look at people, places, and things will guide how we see life itself. And that makes all the effort worth it.

CHAPTER 13

CEILING FANS AND MICROBURSTS

Crap Happens, Find the Humor

Many moons ago, I ended up on the worst date ever. Ever. It was a blind date and it started with being picked up in a vehicle that smelled of old peanuts. And then the gentleman wanted me to hear his favorite song on the way to the restaurant. (Y'all are about to die. I couldn't make this up if I tried.) It was "Candle in the Wind" by Elton John instrumental on bag pipes. And he played it really, really loud. And moved his head and neck dramatically in time to the music. At first, I thought it was a joke and maybe my friends had set me up. But he never turned it off. Then he took me to a hamburger restaurant where we had to pick out our own uncooked meat patties. What?! I almost threw up. Remember, squeamish (they had salads thank the Lord). As we checked out, he told the lady separate checks. Throughout the meal he remained quiet other than a series of grunts. Then on the way home he kept offering me gum. As we pulled back up to my house, he actually tried to lean in. For what, I can't imagine. But I thanked him kindly and basically ran to my door. I couldn't wait to call my friend and ask her was this a test or something.

That's the story of my life. Weird and random events follow me like abandoned Chinese Crested puppies. You know, those strange hairless dogs that whine and make you laugh at their awkwardness. The only choice I have in these moments is to have a good laugh and keep on keepin' on. Because...crap happens. All. The. Time. So, you may as well find the humor in it.

I have a dear friend, Blaire, who suffers the same fate. I have learned over the years that there is an entire tribe of people like us. You may be one of these people. If you answer any of the following questions with a yes, then you are part of the Microburst Society. What's a microburst, you say? I'll get to that. First, answer the following:

1. Have you ever been told, "Things like that only happen to you"?
2. Do so many random things happen to you that people get nervous inviting you places?
3. Have you had to ask yourself multiple times, what are the odds?
4. Do you often start conversations with, "You're not gonna believe this"?
5. Have you been in more than one natural disaster in a day?

If you answered yes to any of these, then you are a part of the Microburst Society.

One Friday I had picked up a car to test drive for the weekend. Late that afternoon I was leaving a client who lived about 45 minutes from our home and I got caught in a hailstorm. By the time I found an underpass to stop at, the storm had passed, and the borrowed new car was covered in dime size dimples. Everywhere. I was mortified. I felt slightly nauseous as I called the gentleman who owned the vehicle and proceeded to send him pictures. He was polite and said not to worry, that's what insurance was for and we could take care of it on Monday. At this point I was running late for a business dinner back in town, so I hurried right to the restaurant. While we were eating our appetizers, I was sharing my earlier adventure. And just as I was saying, "what are the odds of me getting stuck in a hailstorm in a brand-new test vehicle?" the sky outside suddenly turned dark. The wind whipped up and hail the size of golf balls started coming down for about two minutes. And then it stopped as suddenly as it started. I looked out the window at the vehicle that now had tangerine-sized dents and a jacked-up windshield. We all walked outside to assess the damage of our vehicles and noticed that only the vehicles in front of the building had been hit. One of the gentlemen with us was parked further down on the other side of the street and his car was untouched. We were all like what the H E double hockey sticks just happened. And then the realization hit that I had to call the car dealer and try to explain that I had just been involved in my second natural disaster that afternoon.

Later, we found out that we had witnessed a microburst. Apparently, this is a rarely occurring phenomenon. Microbursts can be dry or wet but usually don't have hail. Basically, it's a powerful surge of wind that creates an intense downdraft that can knock planes out of the sky and topple buildings. Kind of like a powerful toot. They can be wet, dry, or include hail.

A week or so later, I was on the phone with Blaire, and she was telling me about something crazy that happened to her involving a glass of wine, a cell phone, and a rug. I told her she experienced a microburst. Then explained my theory on how "rarely occurring phenomenon" or microbursts seem to happen to certain people on a "fairly regular" basis. Including she and I. So now when the crazy random things happen (like falling out of a chair for no apparent reason at a Japanese steakhouse or the time I didn't check my text before hitting send and told my plumber that I couldn't wait to "mate" with him), I chalk it up to a microburst. And in true Brandy Bell fashion I created a make-believe society based on this. (Squirrel: I only refer to myself in third person when I'm doing something weird.)

Sometimes the best thing to do is laugh. Because crappy things just happen. And all you can do is declare a microburst occurred and find the humor. It's pretty therapeutic actually. I find that laughing in the current situation releases more stress than crying. This was especially powerful in the following situations.

I was in a board meeting with a newly established commercial client here in West Texas. We were working on a design proposal for some new offices. During the meeting someone's phone started making some very inappropriate sounds. And no one knew where the sound was coming from. We were all increasingly becoming more and more embarrassed. I was the only girl in the meeting and was mortified and my first thought was, "What kind of people am I working with?" Oh. Wait. Nope. There it is. It's coming from my purse. Unbeknownst to me one of my children changed my ring tone to the part in Forest Gump where he is sitting on the front porch, and the school principal just walked out from "a meeting" with his mom, and he begins making human mating sounds over and over. I was beet red and just smiled sheepishly and said "boy mom." Microburst.

My middle son struggled to fall asleep during his early elementary years because of his ADHD medicine. Sometimes he liked for me to snuggle him and stroke his hair, and count softly, as he went to sleep. One evening he fell asleep in a way that his body was blocking the ladder to climb off the top bunk. I didn't want to wake him, so I tried to sneak off the top of the bed by climbing over the side instead of crossing to the ladder. As I leaned over the rail, I got whacked in the head by the ceiling fan hard enough that it flung me backwards, crushing him, and momentarily knocking me out. (This seems to be a parenting pattern of mine.) Not only did I wake him, but I gave him PTSD. Microburst.

My Round Top trip where I got a box truck trapped under a tree, terrified an entire community, and had to drive a taco-shaped truck six hours to a collision center and swipe my card for $1,500 in damages. Microburst.

Squatting down in front of a crew of contractors not knowing my long maxi skirt was trapped under my foot so that when I stood up, I showed the entire team my ice cream cone undies. Microburst.

Ok, I'll admit it's sometimes a lot harder to find the humor in certain situations. But you still have a choice of how to react either way. In 2018, I had to have an unexpected surgery (I'll talk about "Bert" more later.) There was a mistake made in the surgery and we discovered that's why I was continuing to get sick. And of course, it's a mistake that never ever happens. It was like a microburst of the biggest size. After discovering the reason I was getting so sick after surgery, I didn't laugh, that's for sure. I was pissed actually. But I couldn't hold on to that because I know the anger and bitterness would ultimately only affect me. So in times like that I have to choose to forgive, and find the gratitude. And then later find reasons to laugh. Was it funny that I could have died? Of course not. But now, we are able to look back and find humor in some parts of the story. Like when I left the bedroom overly medicated and answered the front door with no pants on. Hey there Mr. UPS guy. And the time when I was too tired for a meeting at an architect's office to discuss construction plans and my homeowner came to my house dressed in her weird 1970s honeymoon pajamas to make me feel better. It may not have always been easy, but we found reasons to laugh.

Here's what I'm learning: Some microbursts have longer lasting consequences and sometimes they just shake up your day. But how we respond is 100 percent up to us. And sometimes laughter is the best response.

Viktor Frankl, a celebrated Austrian psychiatrist and Holocaust survivor, wrote a book called *Man's Search for Meaning* that has changed many lives, including mine. There are two particular lessons that have helped shape who I want to be.

The first is this: humor is important.

"It is well known that humor, more than anything else in the human make-up, can afford an aloofness and an ability to rise above any situation, even if only for a few seconds. ... The attempt to develop a sense of humor and to see things in a humorous light is some kind of a trick learned while mastering the art of living. Yet it is possible to practice the art of living even in a concentration camp, although suffering is omnipresent."

And the second: attitude is the most important.

"Everything can be taken from a man but one thing: the last of the human freedoms—to choose one's attitude in any given set of circumstances, to choose one's own way."

It is completely up to us how we choose to handle the microbursts in our lives. We cannot control all of our circumstances, only our reaction to them. And I'll tell ya this, I have found it's really difficult to have an angry heart when you're giggling.

CHAPTER 14

BROKEN BONES AND BALLET SLIPPERS

You Choose Who You Say You Are

"You have brains in your head. You have feet in your shoes. You can steer yourself any direction you choose."

—Dr. Seuss

About a decade or so ago I was in a local craft store shopping for trim for a client's pillows when I ran into another designer. She's never been what you would call a friendly sort, but I believe in killing with kindness. We exchanged generic pleasantries and then she asked if I was still painting murals and such. I told her that I was cutting way back because I had too many irons in the fire and I was feeling old. And I had gone back into construction and was trying to just concentrate on interior design work. I laughed and said, "I'm working on simplifying." To which she responded, "Well you're not actually a designer. You're just a decorator." Oh ok. Thanks for the clarification. But she wasn't finished. Then in a haughty tone (reserved for only the truly insecure), she proceeded to tell me about Texas legalities and ASID credentials. But wait there's more. Then she smirked and said, "But I won't tell anyone." Like the design police may come and haul me off.

By now, you know my sharp tongue and sassy wit pop up occasionally. So, I responded with, "I am so sorry that you had to pay thousands of dollars to get a piece of paper to be able to do what God blessed me with at birth." Okay, I'm kidding, I did not say that. My grandmother would have rolled over in her grave. And it would not have been true. Many talented people educate themselves to further refine their gift. To be perfectly honest, I cannot remember what I actually said in response—I think it was an assortment of inarticulate grumblings about puff paint and zebras, and a limp handwave goodbye. But what I do know is it stung enough that well over a decade later it is still fresh in my mind. I think that's what happens when people attack your identity. Whatever that may be.

When we were going through our court trial, my ex-husband said on the stand that I had had a history of abusing my children, as evidenced by their hospital visits. I felt like I had been punched in the stomach. Now let me clarify something. My three boys had in fact been to the hospital a lot. I mean A LOT. So often in fact that I had formed a sort of friendship with one of the intake administrators because we had been in so often. But the hospital never once thought I was at fault. Especially considering most of them occurred in sports and at school. There was the time Andy dropped a large branch from the top of a tree onto Alex's head and he had to have bark removed. The time they put boxes on their heads for protection and shot each other with BBs, and we had to have those removed. Their chins were busted open at the pool and at the school playground. We also had six broken collarbones from football and skateboarding incidents. Not to mention, broken fingers and an assortment of stabbings, including the time Andy used a dagger to chop up ice, and Alex tried to open a toy with a tiny switch blade. And if I can be completely transparent, I was so sick of the hospital that I started patching up anything three stiches or less on my own at home with butterfly sutures. Yeah, I was that mom. My boys were as rough and tumble as they get. But in no way had I ever harmed them. And to be accused of not being a good mom hurt so deeply. Even though I knew it was a complete lie.

Those are not the only times in my life my identity has been attacked. And they will not be the last, I'm sure. I often think the foes we see are easier to disregard than the ones we don't. Sometimes we are the ones questioning who we are.

Have you ever heard of imposter syndrome? Dictionary.com provides this definition: "Anxiety or self-doubt that results from persistently undervaluing one's competence and active role in achieving success, while falsely attributing one's accomplishments to luck or other external forces." Have you ever told yourself that you weren't good enough? Smart enough? Strong enough? Have you ever self-sabotaged even though you knew you were capable? Have you ever attacked your own identity? I have. More times than I'd like to recollect. I think there is some truth to the saying, "We are our own worst enemies."

But here's the amazing thing. We. You and I. Have complete say so over who we are. Every dang bit. You want to be an author? Then do it. Claim it. You want to be a person of integrity and kindness? Then by all means, Choose it. You want to be the world's best mother? Then go for. You get to choose. Not anyone else. You get to be whoever the heck you tell yourself you are. And once you make that decision. Own it. I am a designer. I am an artist. I am an author. I am a builder. And a muralist. And a singer. A talk show host. A dancer. A great mom. A great wife. And a great friend. I am kind. Generous. Educated. Willing. And I am a great cook. Why? Because I said so. Not anyone else. And when I start telling myself otherwise, I readjust and head back in those directions. And since I am writing the definitions, my idea of a great cook and your idea may be totally different. And that's awesome. To others I may not be a great dancer, but when I am out on the floor with my husband two-stepping and looking right into his dreamy eyes, it's my definition that matters!

I probably haven't mentioned it yet, but my feet are shaped like bricks. My parents used to say it would have been easier just to buy the shoe boxes. And I have heard my fair share of Fred Flintstone Jokes. When I was young, I had a dance teacher tell me, I would never be a ballet dancer because of the shape of my feet. They were not made for ballet slippers. Guess she hasn't seen me in my kitchen during the holidays. I'm freaking amazing.

Hey, you want to be an NBA basketball player? Claim it. Your definition may need to include that you are an unemployed, out of shape, non-eligible NBA basketball player, but who cares? Seriously though. No one gets to tell you who you are unless you let them. And there may be some who have earned the right to speak into your identity. Your spouse, family, or close friends. But it's still your choice.

As a person of faith, I have a very set and sturdy identity—and it keeps me grounded. And if you are a person with a similar faith background as me then you know that your identity is secure. And you are beautiful, and gifted, and chosen, because God says you are. And no one can take that away.

Here's what I'm learning: First of all, no one gets to decide our identity. That is completely up to us. We choose. And we have to start by encouraging ourselves. Second, we don't need a piece of paper to define our calling. A friend once told me he has nothing that says he should be doing what he's doing. I relate. I hold no magic paper o' learnin'. I am nothing more than a collegiate gypsy who's taken a long colorful assortment of classes at a plethora of schools from one coast to another. (And I'm not done by the way! I love school.) But I have nothing official that says I am skilled at anything. And yet I still ran a successful design business for two decades. Because what I do have is a love that was placed in my heart from the moment I was fearfully and wonderfully made. And when I was little, I had a mama who let me color in the wallpaper books when she was trying to help design cheesy golf course condos for my dad's business, and a father who didn't spank me when I painted on his blue prints. But most importantly, I have been blessed with dreams and goals and a story. And so have you. Please do not let a title or the lack thereof stand in your way. You may even hold degrees in multiple fields but that's not where your heart is. It is never too late to begin—you just have to take that first step. Own it.

Lastly, we can't let anyone else's negative words hinder us from being whomever we choose to be. Whether your dream is to be the best mom in the entire world or to become CEO of a Fortune 500 company, choose to ignore the haters. And I promise there will always be someone, somewhere waiting with a snide comment or nasty quip. We have to ignore them. All of them. Even the ones related to us.

Here is something that helped me. Find a few moments when you can steal away to a quiet place where you can sit down and write out your thoughts. I used bullet points and then described exactly who I am. (I keep it in a book I will tell you about later.) You can include character traits, job skills, career ambitions, hobbies, things you are and things you want to be. Scriptures. One-word adjectives. This is your definition. Your measuring stick. Your identity. Keep it somewhere that you can easily get to it, for those times when you need a reminder of who you are.

CHAPTER 15

AIRPLANES AND EARTH WORMS.

Don't Let Fear Get in Your Way

"One of the greatest discoveries a man makes, one of his great surprises, is to find he can do what he was afraid he couldn't do."

—<u>Henry Ford</u>

I am not a great flyer. And by not great I mean really, really bad. I used to be a terrific flyer until I ended up on a rollercoaster in the middle of the sky on the way to Atlanta about ten years ago, and all of the screaming and luggage falling about the cabin has created a bit of PTSD in me. And now when any turbulence arises so does my blood pressure. And my body gets hijacked and I start behaving like an absolute crazy person. It starts with my chest constricting. Then I start sweating. Quickly followed by a strong metallic taste in my mouth. And then my pupils dilate and my vision gets super blurry. The cherry on top is my nonsensical, fast paced, slightly emotional chatter, that I direct at whomever will listen and is usually accompanied by unhealthy eye contact for awkwardly long moments with strangers seated near me.

Things that exacerbate the situation:

- The person whose phone is not in airplane mode and makes me want to jump across the aisle and tackle them, because I WILL NOT allow this plane to go down because of their rule breaking!!!
- Mean airline attendants.
- Bad weather.
- The people who are sitting near me sleeping peacefully. What the heck is wrong with them?! I want to shake them and yell "don't you realize we are suspended in midair by NOTHING!"
- Nighttime flights.
- Daytime flights.
- Airplanes.

Also, while I'm on this subject can I just give a PSA? There are certain things people say that just make us "not great flyers" mad. I won't just come right out and call these things stupid, but they are at the very least super unhelpful. So, if you have or do use any of the following, STOP.

- "You are safer in a plane than in a car." Really? Thank you for that unknown gem. You're just a treasure trove of hidden knowledge.
- "Turbulence is just like hitting a pothole if you are riding a bus." OK. Sorry this one is stupid. Busses are not floating forty thousand feet in the air. And if they hit something you don't automatically die.
- "You won't go to heaven until the good Lord is ready." Seriously? I can't even dignify this with a response.
- "Just go to sleep, and when you wake up you will be there." Ok Pollyanna. Don't you think that if this were possible, we wouldn't be clinging to our arm rests for dear life?
- "Just have a drink. It'll relax you." Yeah, tell that to my husband and the flight attendant who gave me four glasses of champs hoping I would stop yelling out in terror on Houston Flight 189.

Yes, I know. I can come across a little brash when I'm talk about things like fear and potential death. I'm sorry. Please forgive me. Here's the thing. I know all of those helpful suggestions are true. But that's the thing with irrational fears. They are irrational. And that's not my most irrational fear.

I am totally afraid of earthworms. Yup. Something must have happened when I was a kid, but I repressed it with all the other junk. Because for the life of me I don't know why they scare me. Do I understand how ridiculous this is? Absolutely. But I own my crazy. If you want to see me run like an Olympic sprinter, dangle one of those little eyeless creatures near me. I am sure you can imagine what problems this posed for a single mother of three boys who like to fish. I have other irrational fears. Being kidnapped in a foreign country and ending up in their prison system. Running out of paper towels. Stickers. Yes, they just get weirder.

With my husband's permission, I have borrowed a section from his book *Course Management* because I love how he speaks on fear with amazing clarity. (The entire book is amazing if I can brag a little on my hubby.) Here is the excerpt:

It has been said that fear is the most powerful emotion known to humankind. More powerful even than love. It is an ancient feeling triggered in the most primitive part of our brain. So, we must learn how to gain the correct perspective on what our perceived fears are if we plan to conquer them and figure out how to use fear in our favor. Imagine what you could accomplish if you learned to harness one of the most powerful human emotions for your own benefit.

First let's recognize that fear often indicates that something big is about to happen. Yes, that can be scary. But it can also be amazing. Choose to believe the latter. Make fear your friend. Allow it to energize you. When you decide to ignore the fears and move forward, you gain mental strength. Even if you fail. You become stronger and wiser when you push past fear and fail. You also become more adventurous and courageous after the battle. Really the benefits of embracing fear are endless and impact every area of your life.

Let me conclude with this. Learn the difference between caution in your gut and fear in your head. You should have caution in unfamiliar situations. And you should have caution if you sense danger (i.e. snakes, tigers, politicians). Listen to your gut. Caution is absolutely exercised in a fearless life. That is healthy. But do not allow fear to override caution and stop you from achieving your goals and enjoying the best life has to offer."

Wow. I love-love-love the thought that when you sense fear, something big is about to happen. That thought helped me through all of the emotions when it came time to finally launch my YouTube show "Sweet Tea on Saturday." Have I mentioned I love interviewing people? Everyone has an amazing story hiding in their hearts. This was something I spent years dreaming about but was totally afraid to do. I had so many fears creep in. *What if no one watches? What if people think it's stupid? Think I'm stupid? What if I'm too old? What if I can't find a videographer? Editor? Money?* It was endless. But I just had to stop worrying about the what-ifs. After years of dreaming, I spent another two years planning and then I took the plunge. And guess what? All of those fears came to nothing. I am older, still scraping up cash to pay tech people, and I don't have a large audience. Actually, as of today I have 57 subscribers. But you know what? I freaking love it.

I also had a dream of starting "Workshoppes" for women. They would have an "All Things Home" theme, and ladies would spend the day with me and a few friends learning things like icing sugar cookies, floral arranging, watercolor, seasonal and home decorating, hosting parties, creating center pieces, packing for trips, and everything in between. And then the fears began. *Who's going to want to pay you? Who are you to teach these things? What if they think's it's a waste of time? A waste of money?* Do you see the pattern? We just have to push through. To this day our So. Bell & Co. Workshoppes are one of my favorite accomplishments. We have hosted them for years and every single one has sold out. I went through a similar process with this book. But you're reading it, which means I didn't let my fear get the best of me.

Here's what I'm learning: Fear is only bad if we let it stop us. But if we learn to use it to propel us forward, it's a mighty tool to succeed. This is yet another thing that I do not have figured out. I'm totally just learning right alongside of you. I still run from earthworms, and I still scare other passengers on planes. But I still fish. And I still fly. So take that, fear.

CHAPTER 16

CRAB LEGS AND CAT BACKS

Hello Humility…and Humiliation

"A great man is always willing to be little."
—*Ralph Waldo Emerson*

O h friends. I cannot count the times I have been humbled. I may even have it down to an art. I can be a wee bit clumsy, occasionally flighty, and well…I am not always paying attention to my surroundings. It's part of my wiring. And I decided long ago that its better just to embrace it.

When I was young, I worked as a cocktail waitress and bartender in a variety of beach towns. With risk of sounding self-deprecating, I went through a period where, let's just say I was far more concerned with how I looked than just about anything else. Before I had kids, I was bar-backing and working the front. But boy oh boy, I could not wait to finally carry a cocktail tray. Because, well, cocktail waitresses were just the cutest. Before I was even legal, one of the managers let me take a cocktail shift because they were shorthanded. Oh my goodness, you would have thought I won Miss America. That night I strutted around like I was on national television trying to win a scholarship. I was ridiculous. I was the exact opposite of humble. Towards the end of the evening I was clearing a table where I had been waiting on a table full of hotshot lawyers and my tiny little blond head was the size of a VW Beetle. I had a cocktail tray filled with about a dozen partially full and empty beer bottles. I was passing through a doorway and just before I walked through, one of the super cute valets said something to me and I lost all focus on what I was doing. As I passed under the doorway, I lifted the tray too high and all of the bottles clipped the top of the doorway, throwing them backwards onto the wood deck and the table that was sitting just to the left of the entrance. The table with two people patiently sipping cocktails waiting to be called in for their dinner reservation. Some of the bottles had emptied their contents and the couple was splattered with backwash. I was mortified. The lady was gagging. The lawyers were snickering. The manager was fuming.

As time passed somehow, I was eventually promoted as a Raw Bartender. (Will these people never learn?) Turns, out I'm pretty likeable. Apparently, my spunky personality overshadowed some of my less developed character traits. One night we were slammed. We had multiple large parties and we were way behind on food. When you are a raw bartender you serve food and drinks, specifically raw and steamed oysters, clams, and crab legs. There was a huge party and I had just shucked about four dozen oysters and steamed another eight pounds of crab legs as apps for this eighteen top. When it was time to run them, everyone was swamped, so me and my grandiose complex decided to deliver them all. On one tray. Yep. You know what's coming. I get about halfway there and as I hoisted up the large oval tray a bit higher, plates of seafood started to slowly slide off the back. It was like gun fire. Bam. Bam. Bam bam bam. Juices were flying everywhere. All eyes in the restaurant were on me. And do you know how many things I dropped after that? About 113,000. It could just be me, but it certainly seems that the more I learn about humility, the more the world gives me to be humbled by. I am either the best student or the worst. Because I am well past 40 and they just keep on a-coming.

One of my lifelong friends started out as a client about 15 years ago. She had gotten my number from another realtor because she had needed some mural work and decorative painting done in her home. We walked out to the garage and she loaded up her darling infant into her beautiful brand-new car. She walked over and showed me how to work the garage door opener so that I could use it to come and go. The opener looked older and she said it was finicky. You had to press the buttons with a lot of pressure to make the doors go up and down. So, she pushed the button on the garage wall itself to open the door. She told me to push the remote button after she exited. I stood there with my palm up, holding the remote like a pie as she backed out. I never touched it. I never touched the remote. But suddenly the garage door started coming down as she was halfway out. I start slamming my finger on the button. "Come on you &%# @ %$! Stop! Stop!" I kept jamming away as I watched the door comedown right on top of the roof of her brand-new car that contained her precious little infant. The universe dislikes me and I don't know why. She braked as the garage door seemed to squeeze her car. And finally, for the love of goats, the dang thing gave up its death grip and headed back up. Now granted this only lasted moments but it felt like an eternity. Shonna hopped out of her car and ran over and grabbed me and looked me in the eyes, and said "Are you ok?" I think I just stood there twitching and drooling and repeating "I never touched it" over and over again. She may have petted my head. I can't remember all of that. But I remember her kindly telling me that it would all be ok and that her homeowners' insurance would cover it. That day she not only drove away with a brand-new car that she had to hunch down in— she drove away with a friend for life.

I learned the greatest lesson that day on humility and humiliation, but not because of my actions. Because of hers. The quote above at the top of this chapter, "A great man is always willing to be little," was exemplified that day through Shonna. She could have chosen to respond in a million different ways and would have been justified for any of them. But she chose to make herself be little right there next to me as I was feeling my absolute lowest. That was her first reaction. That is what beautifully humble people do. And that's the kind of person I want to be. It's a lesson that still resonates in my heart.

A few years ago, I had the opportunity to possibly design a very large commercial project for an oil company that would be a pretty big cherry on top of my career ice-cream sundae. I have never felt so nervous about a project. I was struggling from imposter syndrome big time. It didn't matter how many other commercial projects I had successfully designed—for some reason I just felt like I wasn't good enough for this one. I gave myself more self-talks during that time than probably any other period of my career. I basically had a tiny Tony Robbins telling me how great I was before every meeting. But for some reason my nerves got the better of me each time. For our final meeting to pitch my surface ideas we were going to meet at the airport. They were going to be flying into our city and I would basically have 20 minutes at the airport. I had already been to their Oklahoma offices, so I felt confident that I knew what they wanted and needed here in West Texas, but it did little to settle my nerves.

Side Note—you know how much I love quotes? And definitions? I also love a good adage or old saying. I try to work them into conversations as often as I can. They make me happy. You know, "Cuz if you're gonna be a bear, be a grizzly." See? Meeting these corporate suits was making me "more nervous than a long-tailed cat in a room full of rockers." Okay. I'll quit. "I'm sure you are picking up what I'm putting down." What's important to know about this is at least half the time I mix up the words and get them wrong. Especially the "half dozen one way, six parts the other," or whatever it is. My point is, I like them but usually I mess 'em up.

Anyways…back to my story. As we were at the airport discussing my proposal, they had questions on some specific surface selections. Particularly the solid surface for the entry desks, offices, break room etc. They were not on an unlimited budget, so I went with a level 3 granite. One of the CEOs was wondering why we couldn't use this ridiculously expensive quartzite that his wife had put in their home, that I know to literally be $200 a square foot because I had just used it on a residential project. The solid surface budget for their building was $65 a square foot. Well…I decide now's the time to try out a new saying I learned from my friend who owns a tile store. Because we're all men here right? Yes, be mortified for me. When said correctly the saying is "Higher than a cat's back in heat." I looked at him and said, the Fusion Quartzite is simply not in the proposed budget. And then I followed up with, "Shoot, that's like when I try to stick something in my cat's butt and it's in heat." Yes. Just let those words sit for a moment. I immediately got super flushed and started laughing borderline hysterically. And then they started laughing with me. And all weird invisible barriers and walls came tumbling down. And we had a great time from then on. My friend who owns the tile store and I are still brought to tears each time we retell that story.

Here's what I'm learning. There are a million and one ways to show humility. But the simplest way is to quit trying to impress others and begin loving them instead. In *The Purpose Driven Life*, Rick Warren says, "Humility is not thinking less of yourself, it's thinking of yourself less." Finding small ways to put the needs of others before myself is a practical way that I can be humble every day.

Another easy way for me to practice humility is not taking myself too seriously. I am going to fall. Fail. Flounder. And generally, find ways to embarrass myself. So be it. Not being afraid to make a fool of myself has given me incredible freedom and makes it easy to lift those around me. It doesn't mean I think less of myself, it just means I am perfectly ok with who

I am. And I don't have to try to impress others. When I strive to be humble, I don't feel the need to build myself up all the time. And I like me way better. And when I am feeling insecure and arrogant Brandy shows up, it never turns out well anyway. Also, I always walk away feeling slimy. Another thing I'm learning about being humble is that it makes others feel important and valued. I like that. A lot. And I want it to be a lifetime goal of mine to do my best to build up others. After all, "I may not have gone where I intended to go, but I think I have ended up where I intended to be." That's a great one huh? Good job, Douglas Adams.

CHAPTER 17

BACKSIDES AND BARRICADES

When Life Gives You Roadblocks

"There are no constraints on the human mind, no walls around the human spirit, no barriers to our progress except those we ourselves erect."

—*Ronald Reagan*

Shortly after moving to Texas I started experiencing a pain in my bottom. And by bottom, I mean smack dab in the middle of my butt. At first, I assumed I had just somehow injured my tailbone without knowing. I know that seems unlikely but I'm the girl who regularly has scrapes and bruises and I can't for the life of me tell you where they come from. My husband says I'm hard on life. Not true. Stuff just gets in my way. After a few weeks the pain had increased to the point that I was limping slightly on my right side. I finally made a doctor's appointment. After a series of X-rays, the doctor said the results were inconclusive but because of how the tailbone is situated, you can have a slight fracture and it is not clearly visible. He told me that tailbones take a very long time to heal that I would need to be patient. He offered me a prescription for pain killers (umm…no thank you), and a blowup donut.

It was four or so months later, and I was working at a department store trying to feed three hungry boys and I was having a hard time walking. So…I made another doctor's appointment. The gentleman I went to see didn't seem really sure what to do with me, so he sent me to an orthopedic doctor. A month later, the new doctor also assumed I had some sort of injury as well. Then he set me up with a physical therapist.

Months later, to no avail, the pain was persisting. I was basically limping daily, and I was embarrassed. I think I mentioned my vanity issues previously. To top it off I had to wear dress shoes to work and it was pretty horrible some days.

I went to see a rheumatologist. Again, a series of tests. This guy seemed to be pretty sure right out the gate that I had a condition called ankylosing spondylitis. One of the telltale signs of ankylosing spondylitis is the involvement of the sacroiliac (SI) joints, which are located at the base of the spine, where the spine joins the pelvis. But he would perform a test to see if I had a specific gene, that people with the disease carry. A couple weeks later I'm back at the office and I do in fact have gene HLA-B27. (I had to look that up, by the way. Just in case you think I had it memorized.) So he started me on some sort of biological protein blocker something something. All I know is that it was a pill. (And we know how I feel about those.) A pill I was supposed to take forever. And then another medication called an NSAID for inflammation. But at that point I was desperate. It was getting harder and harder to work and keep up with the boys. And frankly I was sick and tired of being embarrassed by the hitch in my giddy up. Fast forward many months. I'm still in pain, the medications are making me feel gross, and now there are times that the pain is so severe my legs lock up. Next doctor. This time I get sent to a pain management doctor who just wants to prescribe me pain killers. No thank you. I'll just suck it up.

Until I can't. So, this time I go to a family practitioner so that I can tell him what's going on and maybe we can go back all the way back to the beginning and get different tests. He starts asking about my life. My work. My family. My emotions. I think, wow. This guy. This guy right here is really digging deep. Except there are no tests or X-rays. At the end of my appointment he suggested I see a psychiatrist and a good counselor. I walked out confused, and slightly heartbroken.

I spent the next few months in pain and wondering if I was crazy. Or looking for attention. Or both. I began really thinking, maybe he was right. Maybe I was making it all up. Was I like my mom? Oh my gosh. Please, no. I willed myself not to hurt. I would get so mad at myself when the pain was making me limp because I believed I was somehow responsible. So, I vowed to be even happier. I would not slow down. The boys and I would have a grand existence. And I would ignore whatever this was. I would explode joy for goodness sake.

During this time, I had a job change and I also started working again as a muralist and designer. The boys were involved in multiple sports and activities and I was determined, come hell or highwater, that I was going to be supermom. One day after school, the boys were hustling to finish homework and get ready for activities, and I was getting ready for a dinner with my girlfriends. I was walking from the back of the house to my bedroom after getting one of the boys something they needed. My bottom was in quite a bit of pain, but I had learned a trick over the previous months. If I walked on my tiptoes with my thighs flexed, I could barrel through most of the discomfort. However, I was hit with a pain so intense it literally stopped me in my tracks. And I could not get my legs to move without blinding pain. I am not sure how long I stood in that hall holding the wall, willing it to go away. Eventually Andy checked to see if I was ok. I told him I was fine I just had to rest for a moment. But I suddenly needed to use the restroom. But my legs just. were. not. moving. I managed to eek out a couple of baby steps that just about killed me, and as I did, I was unable to hold my bladder any longer. And I soaked my pants and the floor around me. My youngest came down the hall and saw what happened. I was just mortified. And then the other two came along. I stood there sobbing. Not because of the pain. But because I had fought for years to protect my boys and I knew what had just happened would never easily be forgotten. I was broken. That night the pain was so intense, some friends insisted on taking me to the E.R. I was placed in a wheelchair and taken to a room. Again, the doctors had no idea what to do with me. So, they injected me with Demerol and sent me home.

But that accident in my hall that day was a turning point. Because I knew I was not crazy. Never in a million years, in my most desperate condition would I allow myself to put my kids in a position where they would have to see something like that. Never. I was tired of putting on a fake, perky, jovial, brave, fill-in-the-blank face, day after day after day, and at night crying myself to sleep from pain, because someone thought I was seeking attention. And I was tired of trying to hide it all.

There was a period of my life where when people inquired why I was limping, or if I was ok, I would give vague responses, like, "it's an old war wound haha," or, "I just tweaked a muscle working out." Things like that. Shame does that. It causes us to hide. For weeks after the hall incident I stopped pretending I was fine and started asking everyone I came in contact with if they knew a doctor that could help. Enter Dr. C, an orthopedic surgeon who specialized in knees that was highly recommended by multiple friends. He is a bit of a legend in Midland.

Let me tell you about Dr. C. If you crossed your grandpa with the Mad Hatter, and Albert Einstein, you would end up with Dr. C. He had tufts of fluffy white hair, round spectacles, and wore the craziest socks I've ever seen under his dress pants. He spoke with kindness and authority and cussed like a sailor. And I immediately loved him. He asked for me to start from the beginning. Every doctor. Every detail. And I was determined to make it through the entire screen play without emotion, because I was still at the point in my life where I saw crying as a weakness. When I was all done, he asked about my life. My work. My family. My emotions. And then he shook his head, and said, "I'm so sorry. What a long road you've had." And I cried.

The first thing Dr C. said that surprised me was that just because I had that gene didn't mean I had ankylosing spondylitis. He then asked did I ever get a Sed Rate Test. To which I replied, "What's that?" He responded with, "Those dumbasses. That's the first test you do if you think there's an auto immune disease." He ordered a series of blood tests including my Sed Rate and had them the next day.

On my next visit he told me I absolutely did not have ankylosing spondylitis. And that my blood work looked great. I was overall very healthy. So, he ordered an extensive series of X-rays next. And again, all clear. He asked where I had had my MRIs done. What MRIs? And the swearing began again. I could spend all day with this guy. He ordered an MRI for the following week.

When I returned, he said that there was definitely severe inflammation but there were some oddities that he didn't understand. He told me he wanted to run a few more tests and then he wanted me to see his friend that came in town occasionally for work. His friend apparently had the world's tiniest camera and he could get it into places that no mortal man could go. I would be admitted to the hospital, under full anesthesia, but he assured me I would be ok. Two weeks later I am in a hospital bed shaking because I am that terrified. The nurse sensing my nervousness came in and talked to me while they put in my IV. She was lovely and spoke to me as if we had been lifelong friends. She looked at me while they were inserting the needle and said I had the most beautiful hair she had ever seen. I decided she was an angel. I now in fact know that to be true. She and I are still friends. I am not one hundred percent sure how I was still able to hear when I was first in the operating room, but I could hear the Dr. and nurses talking. And the last thing I remember was the doctor. Saying, "Well I've never seen that before."

The next week I had my follow up appointment with Dr. C. to go over the other doctors' findings. And it was the longest week of my life waiting. When you are a creative you have an excess of imagination. Sometimes it's dangerous. (Squirrel: One time I woke Kyle up and convinced him at three o'clock in the morning that there were kidnappers coming to get me while we were in our cottage in Puerta Vallarta. He was even armed with a Conch shell standing by the door ready to pounce the kidnappers as he plotted our escape. I'm not even exaggerating. Turns out it was just our friend walking on the patio above us.) Sometimes our imaginations get the better of us. By the time I finally made it to my appointment I was convinced there were unknown foreign urchins living in my backside. So dramatic.

I sat on the exam table waiting for Dr. C. When he walked in with my chart, he wasted no time announcing, "Well the good news is, you're not crazy. The bad news is you have the ass of an 80-year-old." And I started bawling. Not crying. Balling. Up sucking, snot flowing, shoulders shaking, all out bawling. He started patting my back and telling me it would be okay. I was trying to talk but it came out in a garbled mess. "You, (unladylike noise), don't, (unladylike noise), uh uh understand. (More slobbering and unladylike noises.) I'm soooooooooo happy." And I was. I was officially diagnosed "not crazy" by my doctor. Thank you, sweet little baby Jesus! There was something wrong with me!

Dr. C asked had I ever been in a car accident and sustained injury to my backside. I told him no. He said what was unusual was that I had severe inflammation and break down mainly on the right side of my SI joint which usually signifies trauma. Also, this type of arthritis is reserved for injury or geriatric patients (hence his eighty-year-old-ass comment). It was the most severe case either of the doctors had seen. And certainly not something they had witnessed in a 26-year-old. Consequently, it had caused bone marrow edema and joint destruction that was also affecting the left joint. The cartilage had worn down and those times when I could barely walk were because my bones were actually rubbing together. And basically, my butt was in a mess.

Dr. C said the best course of action for now was to put me under every three to six months depending on how long it lasted and pump my bottom full of things to grease up my joints and take away the swelling. But he was very honest and said this is not something we can do forever. The treatments cause further deterioration over time. I looked at him and said, just help me get these boys raised. I'll worry about the consequences later.

So that's where we began. And for almost four years I received those treatments, and I must say, I know where the term "Miracle of Medicine" comes from now. For the most part I was pain free. I even coached Andy's soccer team during this time. The boys and I called them my three month, 3,000-mile oil changes. They were not easy by any means. I had to have a friend take me to the hospital. I was put under. I was there all day recovering. And then on basic bed rest another day or so. But when I got outta' bed next, boy I was healed! My sweet friend Angie (the one who said Kyle was my type at the concert) was my driver on so many of those visits and would make me her famous banana pudding. Consequently, I relate banana pudding to miracles.

During those years I also tried to do everything I could not to aggravate my joints so I could go longer in between treatments. I became a lover of yoga. I sold my roadster. I got rid of my elliptical machine. I limited my time in heels. And tightened up my family's already strict diet even further.

When my divorce to Mr. Bell finally went through, I lost my insurance and was unable to continue treatments. (I think that was God's way of allowing me to dance later in life.) So, I had to come up with plan B. I started researching holistic medicine and food as medicine like a maniac. And yoga and proper exercise became something I did for my life, not my pants size. This was not an easy journey. There were many setbacks. Like the time Kyle and I were in San Francisco and I basically got stuck in the middle of a road. Where there was traffic. And Kyle still didn't know completely about my little problem. So, what was this crazy blonde doing now? And to this day the boys still poke fun of me if I'm sore and ask if I need grandpa's walker. Heartless turds.

Today, most people who are not in my inner circle have no idea of this journey. Partly because I learned to white-knuckle my way through life, partly because I am not quite as gimpy as I used to be. There are still days when I move slow. Or there is pain in my butt. Or days when I know I need to work from home and rest. But I have not been stuck in bed for years. I believe, first of all, that I have a God who likes to do impossible things. Second, I believe without a doubt there is absolute healing power in what we eat and what we do not eat. I am proof. My joints are proof. I don't think my butt's a day over 58 now. Seriously, there is power in what we eat. I live by the 86/14 rule. Which means six days a week, 86percent of the time, I eat very disciplined. And I follow an anti-inflammatory diet which mirrors the Whole 30 diet in many ways. Basically, that means quit eating all the crap we know is bad for us. Processed chemically drenched food and processed sugar. Meats pumped full of crap. (Ok let me slowly back away from my soapbox and take a deep breath before I scare y'all off.) We try to cook at home most of the time, eat organic, avoid sugar, starchy foods, and limit our dairy consumption. And I have a rule—I almost never eat meat if I don't know where it came from. We try to live this way 86 percent of the time. And some months it may be less. Because we are human. And occasionally the neon sign is proclaiming "Hot" at Krispy Kreme. And I'm probably going to stop, y'all. And when we travel, if there is an In-N-Out Burger, it's going down. And sometimes there is nothing better than a gourmet charcuterie board and a glass of wine with my besties.

Or hot bread with sweet cream butter. Pumpkin cheesecake. Ang's Halloween snack mix with candy corn. Oh my gosh I need to stop. I just salivated on my shirt. The point is no one can be 100 percent all the time. And frankly I think life would be miserable if we tried.

Here's what I'm learning: Roadblocks are often preceded by potholes, uneven payment, speed bumps, construction, roadkill, steep grades, and sharp curves. And sometimes you have to make your way through all of those things before you finally make it to the barricade itself. At that point you have two options: you can take a detour, or you can bust right through that son of a gun. I believe both options are equally effective. And there is a time and a place for both.

Throughout this journey with my 80-year-old butt, I also learned the importance of advocating for myself, of believing myself. No one knows me better than I know myself. It was only when I stopped letting shame silence me that I was able to find the help and diagnosis I needed to live a fuller more pain free life. Sometimes roadblocks are constructed by people who have no idea what they're talking about, and you've got to barrel through those too. The point is to keep going no matter what. We don't want to miss all the good stuff that is waiting just ahead.

CHAPTER 18

SOCIALLY AWKWARD AND SOCIAL NETWORKS

Comparison is the Thief of Everything

"We won't be distracted by comparison if we are captivated with purpose."

—*Bob Goff*

When I was in junior high school, I didn't really know who I was supposed to be. I just compared myself to every other girl in the cafeteria and then tried to mimic them. Because I was so busy measuring myself against everyone else, I never understood that who I was, what I liked, or what I wanted to be, was good enough. It made me socially awkward if I'm being truthful. Sadly, this crept into my twenties. And thirties. And, well…I'm still a bit socially awkward.

Somewhere in my late thirties I realized the absurdity of comparison. My husband and I were in Houston, sitting in a gorgeously designed restaurant complete with four-tiered chandeliers that oozed antique-style crystals. We were enjoying the most delicious seafood dinner that I had had in years. The sea bass was perfectly cooked, seasoned, and with each bite the heavens declared Halleluiah. But I wasn't even fully enjoying it. I was busy psychoanalyzing why my seabass doesn't come out so well. I began chewing every bite ridiculously slowly with my eyes closed. My husband probably thought I was savoring this deliciousness. He may have thought it was sexy. Meanwhile I was trying to figure out what seasonings the chef used so I could duplicate it when I got home. I kept wondering why my seabass never came out as well. Oh. My. Gosh. Well maybe the answer is, because I'm not a freaking professional chef that's why! It was like a little voice in my head said, "hey, ya hardheaded thing, you have no business comparing yourself to this person. Knock it off. And just enjoy." Oh my. Hello paradigm shift.

How much had I been missing out on during my ridiculous bouts of itching from the comparison bug? But just because I figured out I was doing it, a lot, and it was robbing me of all kinds of good stuff, doesn't mean I knew how to quit. It just meant in the beginning I started noticing every time it started happening. And oh holy Hannah. I was basically a comparison addict.

The next place I noticed it was yoga. Oh y'all…you ever done anything stupid while working out because either A. you were comparing yourself to someone you had no right to, or B. you are ridiculously competitive, or C. you have a grandiose complex and you refuse to acknowledge your limitations? Well friend, just label me A. B. C. ya later. Because I suffer from all three conditions. And that day it landed me in a pickle. I did not realize what was happening until I felt my hands go numb and sensed the slight pop in my chest. Because when modifications were suggested for anyone who needed them, my first thought was, "Is she calling me a wimp?" Followed closely by, "Clearly she don't know me." And finishing off the trifecta of unhealthy thoughts was, "If she can do it, so can I." Well Brandy Bell, A. There are 24 other people in this room, what makes you think she's talkin' to you. B. I do know you, and you ain't done a full backbend since you were 13. And C. She's the yoga instructor who has taught in seven countries and is half your age and does this every day. for. a. living."

Have you ever dislocated a rib? Oh my gosh, you briefly believe you're gonna die. I actually frightened most of the girls who were near me.

I wish I could tell you that that was the last lesson I learned on the pain of comparison but it's not. However, I am definitely feeling the sting less and less these days. In *The Power of Vulnerability*, Brene Brown suggests that when you find yourself starting to compare, go into gratitude mode and give thanks for who the person is and what they are doing. What?! Poof. Mind blown. Can you imagine how much more I would have enjoyed that fish had I just had a thankful heart for the chef and his creation? And I am sure my class would have gone way smoother and I wouldn't have ended up with a bill for an X-ray had I simply had a grateful heart for my instructor and all that she was teaching me. Now that's some namaste.

Another coping technique for the comparison bug is to make the person you're comparing yourself to your friend. There is a lady around my age who lives in my town who is beautiful and accomplished and we know lots of the same people. She is a designer AND a fabulous architect, and she has the most beautiful tiny farm behind her home. One day I saw on Instagram that she just published her first book on architecture and design. And I felt that tiny tell-tale prickle on the back of my neck. So, I immediately reached out and asked her to lunch. During lunch, we found out we had lots in common and now we have formed an awesome friendship. If I had let comparison get the best of me, I would have missed out on an awesome sister friend.

There will be limits to this technique. You can't befriend absolutely everyone. Like the guy at the tire shop I secretly envy, who changes my tire in under three minutes and makes me want to become a mechanic. Or every social media influencer in existence that makes me question my homemaking skills. But you can always modify. Being friendly and passing out encouragement is the next best thing. Wow, Billy, you are freaky fast, you should go work for Nascar.

Or, Hey:

@perfectlybeautifulbesthomemakereverinhistory

I love your account. Thanks for the inspiration. Those approaches work great too. Because it's really hard to compare yourself when you're busy making buddies and encouraging others.

No chapter on comparison would be complete without discussing social media. Oy vey. That's a doozy. I still struggle with this one. So, here's what I do. I unfollow accounts where I just can't seem to rein in those feelings of comparison. That's it. Maybe one day I will be so self-aware and self-perfected that I won't have that issue, but it's not likely. So, I hit the unfollow button. The good news is, there are millions of other people for me to be inspired by. So, if I'm so distracted by her perfect donkeys, perfect cherub children, or her perfectly welcoming patio décor, then I need to move on. Life is too short for that.

Here's what I'm learning: It will take a lifetime of therapy and self-discovery to unpack all of the reasons I fall into the trap of comparing myself to others. And while I definitely need to continue my soul examinations with a great counselor and quiet time, I don't want to spend a lifetime missing out. Especially when it comes to relationships. And I think that is where I am especially vulnerable. So, I need to do my best to watch for the signals that I'm about to engage in those unhealthy practices. And choose different paths that are filled with thankfulness and gratitude. This will result in different endings. Endings where I make new friends, enjoy dates with my husband, and avoid E.R. visits. Those are really so much better.

CHAPTER 19

FLYING INFANTS AND THOMAS EDISON

The Definition of Failure

"Failure should be our teacher, not our undertaker. Failure is delay, not defeat. It is a temporary detour, not a dead end. Failure is something we can avoid only by saying nothing, doing nothing, and being nothing."

—Denis Waitley

I used to be afraid of failure. I thought it made me weak. I thought it was not an option. It didn't hinder me from trying by any means. But I was crushed afterwards when I thought the desired outcome was not achieved. Turns out, I was just defining it wrong.

Have you ever watched "Epic Fail" videos? Maybe it's just something a boy mom gets exposed to. My kids have shown me some crazy videos over the years. Bicyclists missing their jumps. Firework displays gone awry. Elephants kicking off their passengers. Tiny babies being propelled through the air. Oh. Wait. The last one belongs to me.

When our first granddaughter was born, Kyle and I were over the moon. Smitten. In absolute and total love. We also treated her like she was made of glass. When Marley was about six weeks old the kids brought her to our home while they went grocery shopping. When they brought her in the house, she was all snuggled up asleep in her car seat, so we thought it best to leave her strapped in, and not risk waking her. I placed the car seat in our recliner, tucked pillows around it, and leaned it all the way in the recline position to create a barrier of sorts. Yes, it was ridiculous. While she slept, we watched a documentary with our two 70-pound rescue dogs, Ginger and Gator. About an hour into our show the youngest Bell child walked in the front door announcing his return from the skatepark. The German Shepherd mix dog jumped up off my lap to go greet him. But instead of jumping straight to the floor he decided to first launch himself onto the extended footrest of the recliner. His detour catapulted Marley about three feet through the air in her seat. And it all happened in slow motion. She ended up no worse for the wear, but I can't say the same of me and grandpa. We were crushed. We felt like we had failed the kids. Failed the baby. Failed ourselves. And we quickly labeled ourselves the absolute worst grandparents. Who else catapults a baby?! The good news is those feelings were short lived. Kyle and I both know that although we certainly didn't have the desired outcome of our mission, we are not the absolute worse grandparents either. And heck…we learned a ton. Dogs can't come in when babies are around. Babies can't be unattended even if they are right next to you. And the Nuna is one heck of a car seat. Also, we learned not to tell the kids if we ever launch a baby again.

I have an obscene number of fail stories I could share with you. I have failed at grandparenting. Parenting. Being married. Being divorced. Being single. Being wealthy. Being broke. Being employed. Being self-employed. I have failed as a mom, a wife, a daughter, a sister, a friend, and a follower of Christ. I have failed at cooking, painting, writing, party planning, homemaking, and everything in between. But it's a good thing.

I can't end this chapter without sharing my favorite (historically accurate) story about Mr. Edison. This is from quoteinvestigator.com, which of course is pure word heaven for nerds like me. And if you like history and language it's a "must" Website.

The anecdote was told by a long-time associate of Edison named Walter S. Mallory. Edison and his researchers had been working on the development of a nickel-iron battery for more than five months when Mallory visited Edison in his laboratory. In his words:

"I found him at a bench about three feet wide and twelve to fifteen feet long, on which there were hundreds of little test cells that had been made up by his corps of chemists and experimenters. He was seated at this bench testing, figuring, and planning. I then learned that he had thus made over nine thousand experiments in trying to devise this new type of storage battery, but had not produced a single thing that promised to solve the question. In view of this immense amount of thought and labor, my sympathy got the better of my judgment, and I said: 'Isn't it a shame that with the tremendous amount of work you have done you haven't been able to get any results?' Edison turned on me like a flash, and with a smile replied: 'Results! Why, man, I have gotten a lot of results! I know several thousand things that won't work.'"

Here's what I'm learning: Everything I had been raised to believe about failure was wrong. Failure is not something to be feared: it's something to be achieved. Failure is how we learn. A life without failure is a life not explored. A life not embraced. A life not lived. Y'all I want to live. I had been told failure was not an option. Wrong. It's the only option. Especially if we plan on accomplishing anything in this world. Raising a family, starting a company, writing a book, losing weight, making friends. We are bound to have a few outcomes we didn't expect. We are bound to have some unsuccessful attempts. That's, how we learn and move forward. We fail forward. All this time I had believed an incorrect definition of failure. At some point I had been taught that the definition began with, "It's bad because." Nope Not True. Not Oxford, Not Webster, Not even "The

Urban"…none of them mention the word "bad" in regards to failure. Failing should be something that happens. Not something that emotionally crushes us. Failing is simply discovering what works and what doesn't. That's all.

CHAPTER 20

PRIDE AND PREJUDICE

What doesn't kill you...

"Vanity and pride are different things, though the words are often used synonymously. A person may be proud without being vain. Pride relates more to our opinion of ourselves, vanity to what we would have others think of us."

—*Jane Austen, Pride and Prejudice*

Super sensitive subject alert.

Because I am squeamish and immature I will from this point on refer to my menstrual cycle as Aunt Flo. Okay then. The first time she came to visit I was little more than a child. She was extremely heavy and stayed longer than she should. This basically continued into my forties. At my first official "girl checkup" the doctor did not show any major concerns and said that this seem to be becoming the norm for my generation. Now when I say heavy, I mean I have had to leave events. And when I say longer, I'm talking 12 days. So, the struggle was real.

When I turned forty it seemed to get worse. At my yearly exam, the Dr. said I should really think about taking hormones through birth control, because my cycles were so heavy and extensive, they were creating fibroids and cysts. Well you can imagine how that ended. Ummm. No thank you.

This lovely pattern continued. One day the pain was so intense I had to cancel my afternoon clients. And then there was the time I all but hemorrhaged at a birthday party while wearing white, and had to clean up "a mess." It was humiliating. And on top of ruining my clothes, Aunt Flo was now dictating my life. Her visits were now so unpredictable that even scheduling a vacation was a crap shoot. But I did NOT want to take pills. Part of it was pride. Part was fear.

And then I had a cyst rupture on my uterus. Oh my sweet potato pie. Talk about blinding pain. Again, my OB said I should try hormones. I told him no thank you, that through diet and exercise I could manage. He kinda scoffed. He should have. I was being a twit. Then he mentioned surgery. UH NO SIR. You just back on up. There won't be none of that here. All of my friends who were tired of their periods were just popping out organs left and right, and I was not going to jump on that train. Nuh uh. No way. I was oozing pride and self-righteousness. There had to be some way to get this under control without knives or pills. There had to be something more I could do. (Are you seeing another life pattern?) My poor husband felt horrible because I was struggling so much, and he just had to sit by and watch. Or worse walk behind me holding a sweatshirt as we left a restaurant. And as the months passed it only got worse.

On my next scheduled visit, the doctor and I discussed a simple procedure that could be done that was minimally invasive and had amazing results. A uterine ablation procedure. I told him I would think about it, but I was hoping not to have any procedures. But I did agree if there was no improvement by my next six-month checkup I would schedule it. I could tell I was kind of getting on his nerves.

By this point, I had begun noticing that my tummy was beginning to look swollen. Now granted, when I had my cycle, my stomach always bloated to the point that zipping my pants wasn't happenin'. But now it was not going away. And I'm not big boned. So, it was getting more and more obvious. Oversized shirts and leggings were my new uniform. One day I was on a work trip in San Antonio and decided to run to the Whole Foods and stock up because we don't have one where I live in West Texas. I was standing in line grabbing a coffee before I tackled my grocery list, when the gentlemen behind me struck up a conversation that would change everything. He was wearing a leather vest with the Harley emblem and a really cool matching bandana. I think he must have been an expert motorcycle rider or something because he looked legit. He also looked like he would win any fight. So, when he spoke it caught me off guard. His voice was soft and kind and a bit high pitched. Like my grandma.

Harley guy- Hi.

BB- Hi there.

H- How are you?

BB- Great. And yourself?

H- It's a glorious day.

Now for me, it was not a glorious day. I was exhausted. Aunt Flo was sucking the life out of me. I was swollen like I ate a melon. And I had a four-hour drive home. So, I just responded with a quick smile and turned around.

Harley guy- You're Glowing.

BB- Excuse me?

H- (Points at my stomach. Smiling.) You're Glowing. How far along?

What. Is. Happening!

How am I supposed to tell this man I'm having the menstrual cycle from hades and that is in fact, my uterus not a baby.

BB- Ummm. 5 months? (I say it like I'm not sure.)

H- *That's great do you know what it is?*

BB- (With more confidence) A boy.

H. *That's really great. Ya gotta name picked out?*

BB- Yes. Bert. (Bert? Bert?! Who the freak is Bert?!) I'm sorry I feel sick, have a good day. (Walking away as fast as I can.)

Are you appalled? I am appalled.

I left that day with absolutely no groceries. But I left with the resolve to see my OB the next day to schedule the procedure ASAP.

After a series of tests, the doctor told me that my uterus was now to swollen and the ablation procedure was not going to possible. I could tell he felt sorry for me. I felt sorry for me. And mad. At myself. He said at this point my only option was to have my uterus completely removed. And he thought It should be done pretty quickly based on its current size. When he told me all that it entailed I almost vomited. Especially when he said I would need to be off my feet for a couple of weeks and that I would need plenty of time to heal. It was imperative that I take things slow. Even my husband grimaced at that. When I was being assembled, God forgot to install my slow button. (And my mouth guard.) I was at the busiest point in my career. I was finishing the largest commercial job I'd ever designed, AND I had eleven other design projects that I was in charge of. I was working nights and weekends just to keep up. And now I was I supposed to take "weeks" off? I sat there tearing up and asked if he could refer me to someone that could also remove a hernia on my naval. I figured while they were taking stuff out I might as well get it done. And, I was going to be off from work anyway right? He looked at me like bats just flew out of my mouth. I said "Go big or go home." When he didn't smile, I quickly explained that it was recommended I have it removed years ago but I hadn't had time. He acquiesced.

During my preop I asked could I please keep my ovaries if they seemed normal. I explained that all of the women in my family that had their ovaries removed were crazy. I also said I didn't want any pain medicine after I left the hospital. The nurse spoke to me very slowly like I was mentally challenged. "You do know you are having a double surgery and one of them requires removing an organ?" Yes ma'am. You can send me with ibuprofen just in case.

Both surgeries went fine. Sort of. They ended up having to put me in a wing of the hospital that didn't normally see OBGYN patients. I was in a ton of pain, but I expected that. I had done copious amounts of research beforehand so I would know what to expect and recovery times. What I didn't expect was a nurse who seemed like she was not sure what she was doing. And I wish she wouldn't have mentioned it was her second day. The doctor came in later for a moment to check on me, said I looked great. He mentioned that my uterus was even larger that he originally suspected. He was holding some sort of pictures. I was still on a slight drug stupor, so they seemed to be moving, like the photographs in Harry Potter. Apparently, Bert was the size of a large grapefruit. Then he pointed to a couple of tangerine sized cysts attached to him. Look honey, Bert's a triplet! Because of this, the surgery entailed more than he initially had thought. He had to make a couple more incisions than projected and the extraction method was a bit more invasive as well. But it all looked great now. The nurse would remove the packing (gauze) later that night. He told me to be sure to urinate as soon as possible so they could release me. That was it. See ya later. Bye.

To condense a very long story, I will give the highlights, more or less in order.

- The brand-new nurse who had never seen an OB patient had no idea how to properly remove the packing. My husband had to call the head of the surgical department (a client) so that she could talk the nurse through the proper procedure with the phone on speaker. Yes. I'm serious.

- I began to get increasingly sicker after the surgery and slept until my post op visit five days later. My husband shared some concerns. At that point I had no idea that he had any suspicions that there was a surgical oops. The doctor said everything was fine.

- I went home and continued to decline. A week later I was still not moving and running a fever. Kyle was concerned and took me back. Kyle asked the doctor to do full exam. He apparently only spent a few minutes checking me over, and again, the doctor said everything was fine. I was mostly delirious at this point, so I have little to no memories. But Kyle said he was very hurried.

- By day 20 post op, my fever had gained strength and I was a puddle of goo. I went back to the doctor with a very high fever. Still in pain. Everything still fuzzy. He ran some tests. Something about my white blood count. I remember hearing dolphins, and him sending me to the E.R. This time my daughter-in-law, who is an ER nurse, came with.

- I got to the hospital, and after a series of tests, they started calling out orders and rushing around. I asked my D.I.L. what was happening, and she said they were treating me for sepsis. I didn't even know what that meant. She said they were worried an infection had spread to my blood. They started IV antibiotics. By the way, all three of my boys were either graduating from high school or college that same weekend and my heart was imploding.

- I am guessing by now you have caught on to what was wrong. Turns out they did not remove all of the gauze.

- Here's the miracle. I will spare you details, but because it was in my cavity, and the human body is AMAZING, my body actually passed it, on its own, after a long excruciating night.

- (By the way, I made to all three graduations. I can't remember it all, but I made it.)

- We called the doctor who performed the surgery to let him know what had happened, but he would not hear a word of it. He just kept saying it was impossible. And he never checked on me again. Not one word. Ever.

- We never felt a peace about pursuing legal action. Some people called us stupid. Especially the med-mal lawyers I work for. But it didn't feel right. We know the nurse who was responsible was young and not properly trained and she wasn't trying to hurt me. She just made a mistake. We all make mistakes. I did contact the hospital and made a formal written complaint so that they were fully aware and could prevent such things in the future.

The morning after my body expelled the "foreign matter," a friend got me into her OB immediately, because he is a friend of her family's. He was kind like Dr. C. was. He started by apologizing for all that I had been through. He went over all the hospital lab work, the X-ray, all of the reports from the surgery itself, and looked at the toilet specimen/foreign matter my body had expelled. He did blood work—I gave a urine sample and he did the most uncomfortably thorough female exam I have ever had. I was there almost two and a half hours. He was calm and said he had great news. My body had no more foreign matter in it. And he talked about how miraculous the human body is. And how mine knew to take care of me by getting rid of what was foreign. I was all proud. I knew my body was good. He then said he had some not great news. Because my body had spent the last few weeks fighting off infection it never actually started to heal. It's called delayed healing. All of the stitches were still there, and it looked like a brand-new surgery. I was going to have to start back from the beginning. No driving. Back to bed. UGHHH. I wanted to know how the other doctors missed the gauze during the physical exam and the X-ray. He said the doctor would have had to perform a full physical to find it, and soft matter doesn't show up on X-rays. He then quietly said, I want to tell you one more thing. I want to explain the gravity of the situation. What your body went through could have actually killed you. People die from septic shock when their body has to fight through overwhelming infection. He then went on to tell me how lucky I was that we caught it so early. But he wanted me to know that my body had experienced trauma and I had to give it plenty of time to heal. This would be a long journey.

I left that day in a whirlwind of emotions.

That was two years ago, and my body is still not 100 percent. But I'm getting there.

Here's what I'm learning: First, stubbornness and pride can be toxic. I'm slowly discovering the difference between healthy pride and unhealthy pride. One is good, and one is very very bad. Healthy pride allows me to maintain certain standards in what I do. That's a good thing. Especially when I'm passing it through the lens of work or my health. Unhealthy pride clouds my judgement and does not allow me to see when those standards need to be modified for my own benefit. In this case it could have killed me. That seems like such a drastic statement, but it holds so much truth. (The pride of the doctor by not admitting something could have been wrong the first visit also played a huge role in the disaster.)

Second, I have to stop making senseless rules for myself that are pride based and include the words, "I will never." It's one thing to say I will do my best to avoid surgery. And another to say I will never have surgery. Or I will never take this...or never do that. These self-limiting rules are senseless and can also do more harm than good. Hopefully as I am learning more, the walls of pride and stubbornness start to fall and I continue to see more clearly. I love what this quote teaches:

"A proud man is always looking down on things and people; and, of course, as long as you are looking down, you cannot see something that is above you."

—C.S. Lewis.

Or, in my case, right in front of me.

Chapter 21

Mindfulness and Melt Downs

When It's Time to Slow Down

"Slow down and enjoy life. It's not only the scenery you miss by going too fast - you also miss the sense of where you are going and why."

—Eddie Cantor

Over the decades of working with my hands, they have occasionally gone through numb and tingly phases. It usually lasts a couple days. Week at the most. But it always goes away. But by November of 2018 my hands had been hurting for about four months, nonstop. And my neck was starting to ache. It had already been a long year of healing from the surgery gone wrong, and I couldn't imagine dealing with one more issue. So, Kyle insisted I go see Dr. H. Kyle is in love with Dr. H. It turns out everyone is in love with Dr. H. When I first went in, I was certainly not loving him at all.

I just needed him to give me some simple exercises that that would help with the tingling and numbness that I had been dealing with in my hands. And the ache in my neck. I mean he could throw in a supplement or two for good measure. I'm always game for a good supplement. But, the first thing he wanted to discuss was my lifestyle. Why are people always wondering about my lifestyle?

I told him I had a pretty intense career—Kyle and I were both very involved in our community and our church. We had five sons, daughters-in-law, two granddaughters, dogs, cats, my mother's bird (may she rest in peace). And on the side, we had our own community organization, hosted workshoppes, a fall marketplace for our community, we both were working on books, a blog, and I was building a YouTube Channel. But that's all. He blinked slowly. Next he wanted to know what I did to relax. I told him I didn't understand the question. He said he was expecting that answer. I wanted to fight him.

Here's the deal. I'm clearly type A. On the Enneagram, I test as a 3 (achiever) and an 8 (challenger) but I pretty much self-identify as a the 3. I have taken about a dozen other tests that also basically say the same thing. "Can't sit still." And it's true, I work best when I'm moving. And taking a long bath is about as close to relaxation as I get. Dr. H. said the first thing he wanted me to do was learn how to relax. But what did that even mean?

For the next hour we discussed my entire life. He wanted to know about my sleep habits, eating habits, exercise, and my workload. Next, he did some testing movements on my hands and my neck. He told me he believed that I had a double crush. Which is a pinched nerve that's trapped somewhere around the shoulders and it's trapped in the wrists. He then went on to tell me that people with my temperament carried all of their stress in the shoulders. Yeah, I hear that a lot.

After another round of questions and tests, he said, "I think you have carpal tunnel but I also think you can work through it. But you will need to make some lifestyle changes. I want you to get nerve tested to be sure." He said he thought my neck pain came from my inability to relax. He then told me I suffered from a lot of stress. I immediately told him he couldn't be further from the truth. I am not a stressed person. I basically radiate joy. He just couldn't see how happy I was because he was pinching my hands, and my neck hurt. He laughed and told me that's not what he meant. (Finally, this guy cracked a smile.) He said, I suffer what's called productivity stress. He explained that my issue is that I never stop moving, physically or mentally. I never give myself down time. Time to renew. Heal. I'm always trying to produce something. That takes up a lot of energy. I told him that was pretty accurate. He told me it was pretty unhealthy. And that it was taking its toll on my body. I agreed and told him that I was learning to slow down. To which he replied, doesn't sound like it.

But I knew he was right. After my forced slowdown from the surgery, I found myself with plenty of time to think in the spring and summer of that year. I was realizing that I had not only spent 20 years trying to sustain an impossible pace, but I had spent most of my adult life proving just how hard I could work and how much I could accomplish. But who was I proving it to, and at what cost? Now don't get me wrong. I still have a healthy pride for those accomplishments. I was blessed to create some amazing things, with amazing people, for amazing people. And I like when my boys say, "My mom built that." I mean my heart swells. But I knew I could no longer maintain that pace. And I wanted to change. About six weeks after my first visit, Kyle and I went on our yearly weeklong sabbatical. Every New Year's we go away and spend a week thinking about the past year and deciding what we want the next year to look like. We talk and journal and dream. That particular sabbatical was course altering for me. Because I knew this would be the year I had to figure out how to slow down. And so I made the tough decision to more or less cut my clients by half. This may not seem like a big deal but we are not independently wealthy. I have financial responsibilities. I HAVE to work. But I knew if I didn't make some major changes I was going to end up in surgery again or in a meltdown. I just had to trust God to provide. (And he did. All year long.) I also decided I would scale back in other areas also. I decided to finish up obligations to any boards and non-profits that year and not commit to any more so that 2020 I could take a break. I also decided that I would finish hosting workshoppes after the fall. As much as I loved them, I had to find ways to cut back. I had to create margin. White space. Breathing room. Whatever you want to call it. And the only way I could see to make it happen was to start cutting branches off the tree. Even pretty ones. Even ones I loved.

I won't give you a full recap of 2019, but I will tell you it turned out pretty good. Although the start was rough. I did indeed cut my projects by half and I cut obligations way back. But let me just tell you something. When you have spent your life going 100 mph and you downshift to 50 mph, you end up with whiplash. Learning not to fill every second of my day was a learning curve. Having available time was confusing.

In March of 2019 I had a client need to reschedule her decorating appointment because of a sick toddler. It was a five-hour block. The old BB would have immediately moved another client up, But not the new BB. I had to figure out how to do things that day but not overfill it. This was still a foreign concept. I started by cleaning my kitchen. But I tried to move slowly. Which makes me laugh now. Next, I decided since I wanted to reorganize my craft cupboards that I could get some new labels. When I got to the craft store, I froze. In my car. In the parking lot. I could not get out. What was I doing at a craft store during the middle of a Tuesday? I called Kyle bawling. He could barely understand me. He kept asking where I was. I was completely blubbering about how I didn't like how I felt, and this is horrible, people were made to work, and "who lives like this!?" In true Kyle fashion, he used his soothing tones and practical suggestions to get me out of the car. He could be an FBI Crisis Negotiator. Clearly this whole change thing does not come naturally to me.

I spent 2019 searching. But it did get easier. To the outside world it may have appeared that I hadn't slowed down at all. But I had. And my family and my sweet husband saw a big difference. I continued to see Dr. H. through the spring. And I think he saw a difference also. My neck was back to normal, and my hands, although still tingly had settled down drastically. And in many ways, I was still busy but my busyness just looked a lot different. I rediscovered my love for making meals for people. And I started painting again. And I discovered that when you leave room for margin and force white space into your life, unexpected things happen. Beautiful unplanned moments spring forth that could never be orchestrated in a planner.

Here's what I'm learning: Sometimes, slowing down looks like stopping. I think it's hard to figure out who you are, and where you're going, when you are moving so fast you never have a moment to think. I'm also learning that when God calls you to slow down, He ain't playing around. I try not to think about the moments I missed and instead I concentrate on all the things I am discovering. Like the amazing conversations you get to have with people in stores when you aren't rushing to your next appointment. And the things I am rediscovering like the peacefulness of my veggie garden and allowing a pumpkin patch to grow. The joy in spending mindless time playing with grandbabies. And staring out my windows at the horses frolicking in the pasture across the street. But most importantly, I discovered I am so much more and the world is so much more than accomplishments and a full schedule. Each day I'm learning that life is richer when you slow down to appreciate the adventure, and not just the outcome. As my granddaughter Marley says, "Sit down. Shoes off."

CHAPTER 22

GOOD DOGS AND GOOD LISTS

Gratitude and Joy

"The root of joy is gratefulness... It is not joy that makes us grateful; it is gratitude that makes us joyful."

—David Steindl-Rast

I f I had to describe exactly how I feel at this moment in one word, it would be grateful. Grateful for where I've been and where I'm going. Grateful for what I'm learning and all that I still need to learn. Grateful that I have experienced poverty and wealth. Grateful for my screwups. Grateful for my wins. Grateful for the family I have and those I have lost. I'm just freaking grateful. For all of it.

This was not always my posture in life. Especially when I was young, and the money was coming in hand over fist. I was selfish and entitled. And broken. Then there was a time before moving to Texas where I had adopted a "poor ol' pitiful me" attitude. The boys and I were lost and struggling, and I blamed everyone else. Gag me. I am glad that was one of my shorter seasons. There were the years that I was so busy concentrating on what I wanted to achieve that I had no appreciation for right where I was. And there have been times in my past when my heart was so crushed that I had a hard time finding gratitude in anything.

I don't have a single ah-ha moment, or an epiphany that I can specifically point out when my heart and mind began to adopt a regular posture of gratitude. I think it was more small steps, that became a habit. And then slowly my character shifted. It's like that age-old saying: "You sow an act you reap a habit; you sow a habit you reap a character; you sow a character you reap a destiny." —M. Wiseman, 1856. I love that his last name is Wiseman. I want my legacy to be: If you sow gratitude, you reap joy.

Bob Goff says, "Figure out what fuels your joy, then do lots of that." An easy place to start is writing it down. Have you ever made a "Joy List?" I read *Saying Goodbye to Survival Mode* by Crystal Paine about six years ago. It is a wonderful book. One of the exercises she has you do, is to create a list of things that bring you joy. It was such a fun and inspirational exercise. And something I highly encourage you to do. Each year I update my list in my journal.

Here are a few things on mine:

- Early morning coffee with my husband.
- Baking.
- Beach combing.
- Afternoon tea.
- Encouraging others.
- Creating things.
- Watercolor painting.
- Hosting dinners.
- Talking out loud to the animals at the zoo.
- Making lists.
- Books.

- Organizing anything.
- Rocking grandbabies.
- All things historical.

My list has like 50 things now. Your list will look completely different. You may write down math. There are actually humans who find joy in numbers. Somewhere. The point is, it's your list. And you need to look at it occasionally, to make sure you are filling your life with good stuff as often as you are able. My life gets crazy still. Family members gets sick. Deadlines loom. Catastrophes happen. Life happens. But feeding my soul with things that bring me joy is a priority.

Making lists is on my "Joy List." So, it will not surprise you that I am going to suggest making another list. I do this one often when I am in the midst of struggle, and joy seems to be eluding me. I write down the things I am grateful for in that moment.

We recently went through a heartbreaking custody battle over one of our granddaughters. There were nights that I cried myself to sleep. My heart was so broken that it physically hurt my body. And every day I decided I would choose joy. And the only way I knew how to do that was to find what I was grateful for. I wrote that I was grateful for her health. I was grateful she had so much family to love her. I was grateful for my son who has the heart of a lion and learned to fight like his mama. I was grateful to my husband who loved this little girl with every ounce of his being, even though there was no blood relation. Because being a granddad is one of his greatest joys. I was grateful for our justice system. I was grateful for America. I was grateful for our lawyers and their hearts for this little girl, and my friend Michele that allowed me to vent every single day. When I was at my most broken, I just sat in the rocking chair crying to God and thanking him that he created her. Over and over.

In *The Book of Joy*, Desmond Tutu says this: "Discovering more joy does not, save us from the inevitability of hardship and heartbreak. In fact, we may cry more easily, but we will laugh more easily too. Perhaps we are just more alive. Yet as we discover more joy, we can face suffering in a way that ennobles rather than embitters. We have hardship without becoming hard. We have heartbreaks without being broken." I love this.

Here's what I'm learning: joy doesn't come from calm waters and perfectly smooth sailing. Joy comes from being grateful, regardless of what the sea may bring. It is a discipline that I have to choose. Every single day. And that's not easy. But my life is so good and there is so much to be grateful for. I can't imagine how I ever lived any other way. This decision to choose joy everyday has changed my life so radically that I have already started a series of mini-books and the first one is on joy. And yes, I have already started a second book and I have no idea if anyone is going to buy this one. Sometimes you have to put the cart before the horse. So, if you are reading this, especially this far in. I am sincerely grateful for you my friend.

CHAPTER 23

SOUTHERN BELL AND COMPANY

What Do You Want To Be When You Grow Up

"Every great dream begins with a dreamer. Always remember, you have within you the strength, the patience, and the passion to reach for the stars to change the world."

—*Harriet Tubman*

When I was little, I told my parents I wanted to be three things when I grew up. An archeologist that studied ancient Egypt. And artist. And a veterinarian because I loved animals and I wanted to set my own hours so I could be a single mom. Apparently, I never mentioned a husband, so there's that.

I think we need to pay attention to what we dreamed of when we were little. There are lots of clues there, that we decide at some point are no longer important. Clearly, I did not become an archeologist. But I have taken countless courses and have spent years listening to and reading anything I can get my hands on about Egyptology. I am just waiting for some university, somewhere, to reach out and offer me an honorary Doctorate as an Egyptologist. But even if they don't, I am totally still one in my heart. And that counts too. One day I will visit all of the places I study. As soon as I start practicing what I preach and deal with two of my largest and most ridiculous fears. Flying and being kidnapped in a foreign country. In my head Egyptian jails are especially gruesome, so I may wait until I'm old and they think I am too decrepit to arrest.

I am also not a vet. But I still love animals. All of them. We live in a neighborhood that is broken up into agricultural estates. Our property has several large barns and fully equipped stables. Guess how many farm animals I have? None. Zip. Zero. Saint Kyle seems to think that I travel too much and he will be left to care for them. Not fair. We already have two dogs, four cats, a bird, a turtle, and a squirrel with no tail, what are a couple mini donkeys in the big scheme of things? And maybe a fainting goat. And one llama. Possibly a monkey. But that's all. I swear. But because he is holding his ground, I have resorted to roaming the neighborhood every few days and talking to everybody else's farm animals and horses. I am sure my presence is somewhat unsettling to the neighbors who still don't know me. Random lady, dressed in mismatched yard clothes, hanging desperately onto their fences, crooning in baby talk for their animals to just come and love her.

The artist thing I am still working on. In some ways I have had a good run at it. Design and decorating are a form of art. Murals are basically large art. And commissioned work is for sure art. But it's not what I was dreaming when I was five. And, I'm not ready to give that up yet. I am super grateful for an amazing career that has provided for my family, but I still have plans. In my heart and head. I want to produce the art that I want. My own vision. I have spent two decades doing my best to get out of my hands what is in other peoples' heads. Now I'm ready for my hands to produce what's in my head. I have some plans brewing, and frankly it's all very exciting.

I think it's super hard to figure out what we want to do, and who we want to be, when we never stop and think about it. Or dream about it. 2019 was the year I decided to take that seriously. Having margin in my schedule left me time to dream again. When was the last time you dreamed about what you want to be? In Tim Ferris' book, *Four Hour Work Week*, he challenges readers to daydream about what they would do if they had unlimited talent and money? Sit with that a moment. That's intense huh? I encourage you to try this. Find a quiet place, grab a note pad and daydream. Then write it down! Other questions you can ask yourself to discover those dreams: What breaks your heart and what makes your heart sing? What makes you fiercely passionate? Who do you want to help? What do you want most and what are you willing to give up making it happen?

I think our dreams definitely change as we grow older but there are still some childhood seeds planted. I no longer want to be a vet. It doesn't even appeal to me. And I don't want to spend my days working as an archeologist either. But that doesn't mean I cannot find ways to make those things a part of my life. Dreams don't just have to be things you make money at.

As we grow and have new experiences life adds dreams to our hearts also. For years I dreamed of finding a way to help and encourage single and working moms. After all that I had journeyed through, it was almost as if that dream became seared to my soul. But I had absolutely no idea what that looked like or where to begin.

The year before we moved to the "Little Teeny Farm," or "LTF" as we dubbed our property, I had one of those moments when life tends to stop you because it has something to say, and you won't sit still. I woke up one morning and had absolutely not one ounce of energy. I mean none. I didn't feel sick. There were no other symptoms, but I could not move. It had never happened before and has not happened since. I told Kyle that I was going to cancel my appointments and sleep that day. I fully intended to just go back to sleep. But I couldn't.

I was exhausted. But absolutely unable to sleep. So, I laid there awhile reading. Until I felt prompted to grab a notepad and start writing. And that day Southern Bell and Company officially became a thing. I have always kept a spiral and jotted down thoughts as they came up, or business ideas. And I had played with the name for years, and even brainstormed all of the things I could do. But I had never really done anything with it. And through it all, I had been praying fervently for God to show me how to help others. And that morning began a journey that is still continuing to this day.

I spent that entire day in bed making plans and taking action. I had no idea what I was doing. I just knew I was supposed to be doing it. I had thought up the name years earlier, thinking if I ever had a large business, I wanted it to have fun southern traditions and include lots of people. So, I had first wrote down Southern Bell and Friends. It sounded a little juvenile. The concept of "Company's Coming" was always important to me, so I changed it to Southern Bell and Company. Or So. Bell & Co., as we refer to it now.

I texted my friend Jake, a super talented graphic artist, and asked for his help. I sent him the name and a round logo I had designed before. Then I went and bought up the domain names both for the full name and the abbreviated version: sobellandco.com. I started an email, and all the social media accounts I could. Since I still had no real idea of what it was, I just started writing down what I wanted to be. And it started pretty vague. I wanted to encourage women. Host events. Help single and working mamas. Make pretty things. Have fun. Write. Create. I even decided what colors, smells, and vibes would fill the world of So. Bell. & Co. By the time Kyle came home that night, I was still in bed, but glowing. I was like a ball of sunshine wrapped in white bed sheets.

Since then So. Bell & Co. has grown and evolved into something that is beautiful and filled with people. When I'm asked what it is, I still fumble over my answer. Because I'm not 100 percent sure. The short answer is community. The long answer is workshoppes, and women's events—a fall marketplace where we have 30 mom vendors selling the things that they created, to help raise money for the other moms and kids in our community. It may be one woman in my keeping room, or a hundred women at a conference, all with dreams that seem so big they dare not tell others. It's dinners and celebrations at the LTF. It's videos and blog posts. Retreats and art classes. Its laughing and crying. And now, it's this book. I'm thinking Southern Bell and Company is less of a what, and more of a who.

Here's what I'm learning: there is not a statute of limitations on dreaming. It's something we are called to do until we rest peacefully in the ground. Or in the Atlantic Ocean in the case of my family. I'm learning that dreams don't have to be perfectly defined to begin. As with So. Bell & Co. some dreams need permission to grow and develop on their own. I'm also learning that some dreams are just practical ambitions. Cash flowing all my kids' college expenses is a dream of mine. And because some dreams involve others, my sons play a part too. Some dreams are simple but take years of investment, like being able to do yoga when I'm 80. And some dreams are complex but require faster solutions, like owning a company that provides income for mamas that need help. The biggest thing I am learning is that the answer to the question, "What do you want to be when you grow up?" may have nothing at all to do with your career and everything to do with the people around you. In my case, when I grow up, I want to change the stars for those who cross my path.

P.S. Don't wait for life to trap you in bed to get started.

Here are just a few amazing authors who have helped pave the way for millions of dream chasers who may inspire you.

Mark Batterson. Tim Ferris. T.D. Jakes. Jo Saxton. Emily Vey. Gary Vaynerchuk. Bob Goff. Priscilla Shirer. John C. Maxwell. Jess Connolly. Jon Acuff. Brené Brown. Simon Sinek. Annie F. Downs.

CHAPTER 24

BULLET POINTS AND LADY GRANTHAM

Living Your Best Life

"A goal without a plan is just a wish."

—*Antoine De Saint-Exupery*

I believed for a long time that if I worked hard enough, I could control the outcome of everything. Add to that, sadly, that I even tried to control others. All well intentioned I assure you. I mean bless their hearts. They needed my help. Have you ever wanted to go back and tell yourself to go pick out a switch? Learning the reality that the only thing I can control is my own actions, is still a long bumpy process. But I'm definitely improving. It was obvious the more I tried to control life with my Jedi death grip (is that a thing?), the more out of control everything seemed...and the more out of control I began to feel. Something had to give. And it began with me stepping back and taking a good look at where I was and what needed to change.

I love to journal. I don't long form journal. I bullet point. It's like making lists of my thoughts.

Aug. 14 2016 * Today kinda sucked.

Sept. 1 2017 *Ginger hurt her paw.

See? Simple. Anyone can do it. But over the last decade my personal journal has evolved. And now I have a full-fledged accountability book that houses my goals, my priorities, my dreams, my joy list, and a whole lot more. Okay, please don't check out. Please. Please. Please. Because this is a tool that has helped drastically shape my life and it has been absolutely invaluable.

Let me start by saying I believe that a great life is made with teeny tiny steps in the direction you want to go. And it is a fact that when you write something down you are more likely to accomplish it. This is not a cliché. Its neuroscience. So, I believe, in order to see real and lasting change you have to write it down.

I am not going to waste time telling you the evolution of how I went from simple journal to accountability book, because I don't want to lose any of you in the details. I believe this is that IMPORTANT. So I am just going to describe what is in mine and how I use it. You can make yours as simple or involved as you would like. But the most important thing is to make it your own! This is about intentionally living the best life you can. John Maxwell writes in his *Intentional Living,* that "Nobody finishes well by accident."

To start off with, my book is a simple five subject spiral notebook that I added divider pages with pockets to. But I have used traditional journals, and three-ring binders also. I just found I like the way the spiral feels and the pages rip out less. If you are super creative, the art supply stores have a variety of interactive customizable journals. They are lovely. However, mine only cost four bucks at Target. Also, this is not my day planner. It's not a scheduler. I know there are some amazing companies that have combined the two, but I need a bit more space than their goal setting sections offer.

However, that might be a great alternative if you are just starting out. Inkwell has a great day planner with goal setting sections.

I need to also let you know that this is what I spend my time doing when we take our sabbatical at the end of each year. I spend two or three days on mine. You may not have the ability to invest that much time. And that's okay. Remember this is not about you doing it all at once. It's about starting. And that's often the hardest part.

I prefer a blank Cover so that I can write the year on the front. I also write my word for the year, my quote, and my scripture. They act as an easy reminder of the direction I want my life to go. For instance, my current one says: <u>2020. Be.</u> <u>"You don't always need a plan. Sometimes you need to just breathe, trust, let go, and see what happens."—Mandy Hale.</u> And, <u>"Be still and know that I am God." Psalm 46:10.</u> Obviously I am trying to intentionally slow down and be intentional in 2020. I didn't say stop. Just slow down. Breathe. Be.

I divide my book into four sections with pocket dividers, because I find I like to keep things that I pick up along the way. Little reminders.

My fear right now is that some of you are so intimidated you won't start. Again, my way is not how you have to do it. I spent 10 years designing my strategy. You could start with a simple seventy-five cent one subject notebook where you write down what you would like to accomplish for the year, and two or three priorities. That in itself is powerful. Maybe you adopt part of what I do or maybe you design your own from scratch. It is whatever you need to hold you accountable, to live your best life.

Here is how I have my Accountability book/journal laid out:

There are four sections:

Heart. (Emotional)

Soul. (Spiritual)

Mind. (Mental)

Strength. (Physical)

I have them sectioned this way, because I believe people are made up of these four parts. Every section includes my priorities and goals for each area. Think of priorities as the "whats" and goals as the "hows." For example:

Priority- To maintain flexibility as I age.

Goal- Take two yoga classes a week.

My "Soul" section includes:

- My spiritual priorities.
- Simple steps (goals).
- My prayers.
- Favorite scriptures.
- Favorite notes from podcasts and sermons I listen to.
- And I tend to tuck things in the front pocket that remind me of times God has been faithful, or church handouts from churches I have visited while traveling that year.

My "Heart" section includes:

- My emotional, personal, family priorities.
- Goals for each area. Family, friends, community, financial, personal, career, etc.
- I have a copy of my core values. I think writing out our values is an important first step in deciding what direction we want to go.
- My personal constitution, some people call this a personal mission statement. Steven Covey, in *Seven Habits of Highly Effective People*, has great examples and help with accomplishing it.

- I have my "Joy List" that I mentioned in Chapter 24.
- I have a list of mantras, meditations, I like to repeat during high stress situations.
- I have a page where I wrote out my "Why." Simon Sinek's, *Start With Why* was pivotal in putting my heart to words. Game changer.
- Quotes that inspire me.

My "Mind" section includes:

- My mental and educational priorities.
- Goals.
- I like to write each book I read on its own page. That way I have a place to add little nuggets that I learn, and I can reference back when I need to.
- Notes from podcasts.
- Notes from conferences.

My "Strength" section includes:

- My physical and health priorities.
- Goals.
- I write down small wins.
- You could also use this section as an exercise and food journal.

Again. I cannot say this enough. This is about you. You lay your journal out however it will best serve you. You can have one section or 50.

Also, this is not a one and done either. I don't write in my book, put it in a drawer, and hope it magically changes my life. I keep this thing close by. I throw it in my car during the day and bring it in at night. It travels with me also. It's like a pet. Ohmygosh! I should start naming it each year. Okay. I am naming 2020's book "Lady Grantham" after my favorite Downton Abbey character. She's wise and witty. A wee bit sarcastic and she moves slow. Totally fits the theme of where I'm headed! Ok, let me get back on track. (The squirrels are extra rambunctious today.) I keep my book with me for a reason. If I have a great thought, I can write it down. If I go somewhere and have a cool trinket like a conference ticket or a card of encouragement from a friend, I put it in a pocket. If God speaks to my heart, it goes in my prayer section with the date. If I am stressed or having a hard morning, I have pages of encouragement to turn to. But there is something even more important I must do. Once a month I check in. I usually find a quiet hour on a Saturday around the beginning of each month, grab a cup of tea and check in to see if I am on track. And I loving my people well? Did I start working on that goal I wrote down? Am I following my exercise regimen? Essentially, am I being consistent and doing what I said I was going to? This is vital for me. After all, it's my accountability partner. OK wait. Bear with me. This is just too good to resist. It just dawned on me that Lady Grantham is my accountability partner and once a month we have hot tea and talk about my life. Oh happy day.

The last thing I do is review it the following year before I start my next one. What items need to roll over because they still need some time and dedication. What cool things happened during the year? What prayers were answered? What have I gotten better at? It's honestly a lot of fun. And whatever I think needs more time I just move into the next book. No judgment. You guys…I have been rolling over "watch my potty mouth" for 10 years! Because just when I think I got it down, my salt comes back twice as thick. But I have seen so much improvement also. I love having a record of my growth.

OK. I need to throw in two more things. 1) This book is not to replace a human. You also need two or three people that love you and can help live into your life. And 2) Don't hold it so tightly that you feel like a failure if you are not getting an A+ in every single thing. My 2018 was so rocky that when 2019 rolled around Instead of starting a new book I literally added the words "And 2019" right next to 2018 on the cover, because I felt like I needed a repeat. That's life. And grace. This is to guide you, not condemn you.

Here's what I am learning: I cannot possibly be a better version of myself without a vision of what I want that to look like. This takes time and intentionality. And I have to have grace for the times that I don't get it right. And they are often. If I want to accomplish things that are important to me, I have to be intentional. And I have to have a plan. There is no other way. If I want to be a good mom and wife and friend, I need to know what that looks like for me, and then make sure I am doing the things that I need to. Lastly, I am learning that the more I grow the more I enjoy this beautiful, messy, off-the-rails life that I have been blessed with. And I hope you find the same thing to be true for you.

CHAPTER 25

GOOD WORDS AND BAD WORDS.

You are what you think.

*The happiness of your life depends upon the quality of your thoughts:
therefore, guard accordingly, and take care that you entertain no notions
unsuitable to virtue and reasonable nature.*

—Marcus Aurelius

I can't tell you exactly when I developed my fascination (insert—obsession) for neuroscience, but if you get me talking about it at a party I use the same voice I use when I'm talking about my donkeys, Disney Movies, or King Tut. It's my jam. It's also been a catalyst in changing the way I live my life. So, forgive me while I nerd out on you for a bit. Because what I'm about to share is huge.

Did you know that you have the ability to actually change the way your brain works? It's true. There is a Dr. who I follow named Dr. Caroline Leaf. She is a communication pathologist and cognitive neuroscientist with a Masters and PhD in Communication Pathology and a BSc Logopaedics, specializing in cognitive and metacognitive neuropsychology. Basically, she's really smart. She has shown that our DNA actually changes shape in response to our thoughts. That is worth repeating. Our DNA changes shape in response to our thoughts. What does this mean? We have the ability to change our thoughts and create new lines of thinking. We can retrain our brains. And that changes everything. It's called neuroplasticity. Our brains are moldable, malleable. Neuroplasticity is our brains ability to adapt and change. The old adage: "You are what you think." It's not a cliché. It's proven science.

All of that negative self-talk we engage in? Yup. It programs our brain. When we are having those moments of insecurity where we tell ourselves "we can't, or we are not worthy"… we are in fact sending signals to our brain. And when we speak those things out loud, it's a double whammy. You just gave your brain twice as much information to use for reprogramming. The definition is neurolinguistic programming. It has the potential to mold and sculpt our consciousness because our minds are malleable.

The good news? The opposite is true also. Have you ever been to a conference or an event and they want you to repeat things out loud? Or worse, say them to the total stranger sitting next to you? I am getting neck prickleys just thinking about it. Have you ever read a book and the author wanted you to go find a mirror and tell yourself a positive message? I used to think that was creepy. But I'm sippin' the sauce now. I once visited a historic southern Baptist church where the pastor, a beautiful African-American man with the kindest eyes I have ever seen, had us preachin' right along with him. He would say something, and then tell us to shout it out. It was so much fun. He had us repeat "Today's gonna be a good day." Over and over. Louder and louder. And ya know what? I'm pretty sure I had the best day ever. By the way, if you ever have the opportunity to listen to a full southern gospel choir, you will get a glimpse of what heaven surely sounds like.

Just like negative self-talk and messages rewire your brain, so does positive self-talk and messages. In *Power of Vulnerabilty*, Brené Brown talks about mantras. I love mantras. I have a page of them written in my accountability book. I believe in them. I use them at events and parties. Before I speak, and before I film. When I meet new people. When I'm nervous. And I often use prayers the same way. I keep them short and sweet. One of my go to's is, "Oh Lord, fill me like smoke." This is great for when I am feeling fear. Or I want to show kindness to someone who has hurt me. Or when I am standing in line, at the grocery store at 10 on a Saturday morning, and the person behind me is yelling into their cellphone.

Whether you call them mantras, meditations, prayers, or self-chats, they hold the same power. They can change the way you think. Forever. And guess what—that changes your life sister. Also, if you couple any of these with deep breathing, it's like adding gas to a fire. The brain is oxygen dependent, using 20% of the body's oxygen supply. There are countless great articles on the science behind oxygen and our brains and the research is growing everyday. So, what do you do with this information? Well. You breathe. When I am saying a mantra, or a prayer, or meditating, I take slow-deep-belly breaths. And it changes my posture instantly. Give it a try. Make it a habit. And notice the change.

So, what happens when the negative thoughts or words pop up? And they will. Well, you change them. We have the total ability to redirect them. I still catch myself saying things out loud occasionally. Like when I have made a mistake or done something I perceive as silly, I'll say, "Oh my gosh, I'm so stupid." It's been a habit for years. Do I really believe I am stupid? No. But, is it healthy for my brain? Absolutely not. So, after I say it, I follow up with. "That's not true. I just made a mistake." And if I am alone and feeling particularly saucy I may add, "I'm pretty dang amazing."

The science of neuroplasticity also goes hand and hand with how we handle life situations. We may not control the circumstance, but we control how we react to them. And how we react to them affects our brain. Neuroplasticity.

And for my faith family, neuroscience is found all throughout the word. My favorite being in Philippians 4:8 (NIV): "Finally, brothers and sisters, whatever is true, whatever is noble, whatever is right, whatever is pure, whatever is lovely, whatever is admirable—if anything is excellent or praiseworthy—think about such things."

Here's what I'm learning: I have the ability to alter the direction of my life because I was born with the ability to make up my mind. What I tell myself is going to impact not only the way I handle my life, but how I handle my people, and every situation I find myself in. So, it is my responsibility to fill my brain with the good stuff. And you know what? I have found that when I decided to start doing that, I changed. In so many ways. And it turns out, I am intelligent and deserving. I am capable and equipped. I am funny and creative. I am destined for great things and I will not be afraid to fall. I am beautiful, loyal, excellent, and worthy. Why? Because I said so.

CHAPTER 26

MELTING SNOWMEN AND FALLING LEAVES

There is a Season

"I hope I can be like an autumn leaf.
To know when it's time to cling to the tree,
when it's time to change colors,
and when it's time to fall."

—*Me*

I tend to cling to certain seasons. Not always recognizing when it's time to change. A prime example of this is the raising of my boys. I tried so hard to keep them little that I looked up one day and they were becoming men. And I had missed some of it. Instead of embracing and enjoying that journey, I missed out on some good stuff because I was looking the wrong direction. I was so worried I was losing them that some of the moments that mattered were gone. It's something I still mourn. But it's given me the determination not to miss any more.

I had to learn that lesson early in my career also. When the boys were young, I set some pretty high career goals. One of them was making a certain number of zeros before I turned thirty. I thought I had something to prove and I wanted to show my boys that they could accomplish anything with hard work. The goal itself was not inherently wrong, but I never once stopped to consider whether that was the season of life I should be trying to accomplish that goal. And I should have checked my motives. I accomplished the goal. But at a cost.

When you study the seasons, you find that they are ALL necessary and that they all have an important purpose. In the Spring the ground is fed. In the Summer the ground produces. In the Fall the ground is cut back. And in the Winter the ground rests. They are all important. And the seasons in our life are equally important. I lived my life in an endless summer for longer that I care to admit. I think that's why the Winter did not come in like a flurry, it came in like a blizzard. And I was trapped inside. And guess what? I am so very thankful now.

I believe I have a bit of catching up to do in order to level out the imbalance. I just spent the most beautiful ten months in November. I slowly cut back and pruned lots of areas. And I took a deep breath and looked out at the leaves changing on my trees. After my extended Autumn I crept into Winter and lingered for a while. And now I see Spring peeking around the corner, and I plan to stay there for a while also. And feed every square inch of my neglected ground. And y'all, there are a few bald patches that have been hidden in the shade that need extra fertilization.

This is an exciting season for me. I think the Fall, and the Winter, and the Spring provide perfect conditions for dreaming. Planning. Discovering. Figuring out what I want to be when I grow up. I am rediscovering some old things and making plans for some exciting new things. And it's an adventure I'm savoring.

Here's what I'm learning: We need to embrace every season of our lives. There is a time to slow down and care for our littles, and a time to hustle and kill it in the goal-setting department. There is a time to rest and feed our souls, and a time to fight for that dream hiding in the depths of our hearts. There is a season to feed ourselves and to feed others. The important thing is that we don't stay in one season so long we miss the beauty and the growth that comes from the others.

Snowmen melt in the spring for a reason. I have to be aware of when it's time for the seasons to change. And then have the courage to move into the next one. All seasons are beautiful and have so much to offer us. And as I am moving into the next season of my life, I will be brave and curious and intentional. So that, when the time comes, I am ready to bloom.

CHAPTER 27

THE BEGINNING AND THE END

My Reason Why

"Blessed is she who has believed that the Lord would fulfill His promises to her!"

—Luke 1:45

I went to a leadership conference with Kyle a few years ago, hosted by a gentleman named John C. Maxwell. It was a very long very informative three days. We were in our last large group session. I am guessing there were 3,000 people in attendance. At the end of the teaching John stood up and announced that there was one more small session. And this was the one where he shared his faith. But he also announced a bathroom break. And told everyone who did not feel comfortable staying that they could go to the restroom, unnoticed—and they would not be judged by him. So, this is where I say the same to you. This has been a long journey, friend. Thank you so much for sticking with me. I am now going to share my "why" with you. I will not try to convince you of anything, I just have one more story to tell. And If you are uncomfortable, please head right on over to the restroom...I mean the conclusion. You will not be judged by me friend. However, I hope you like my brand of crazy enough to keep going. Because I think the last chapter is the best part. And I would not be true to who I am if I didn't share it with you.

I grew up in church. It was my family's church. I loved it. I especially loved Vacation Bible School. Because we made tons of crafts using magical supplies like popsicle sticks and paper plates. And at the end of the week there was a special program. Following the program there were refreshments in the fellowship hall. Surrounding the walls were tables with all of our crafts displayed. I could not wait for my parents to see what I created. I loved that little church. I learned the Bible story's and felt safe. I learned beautiful hymns and the Apostle's Creed. But somehow, I missed the part where I was supposed to know Jesus.

As my life progressed, I would occasionally pop into a church wherever we were living, but mostly out of habit. And I wanted my kids to be raised around church as I had been. I can't say it was helping my mess of a life, but it always felt safe and familiar.

When I moved to Texas, I did the same as I always did and looked for a church. When I heard of one, from someone shopping at the department store I was working at, that had great kids' services, I jumped at it. At the service I attended, the pastor was preaching on marriage. And he said "Husbands, don't expect your wife to submit, if you're a jerk." And I was like who is this guy? So, I started attending every week. And then I started attending Sunday school. Next thing you know I was volunteering. The people were kind, the sermons were more like life lessons, and my kids were happy. Besides, I got free daycare for three and a half hours every week and received a much-needed break. Remember, new in town, no friends, no family, no money. And I have three little boys in tow. I needed it.

One particular week the pastor gave a message on being enlisted in the army. Everyone in the choir dressed in camo. The preacher came out in steel-toed boots, and there was an army jeep on the stage. They passed out a handout and it had a space at the top where you were to write in your enlistment date. Well I didn't know what that meant. So, after service I asked my Sunday School teacher's wife. She asked me when did I accept Christ as my Savior. I told her my parents were Christian. I was born Christian. And I had been sprinkled as a child to seal the deal. She told me that you are not born with Christ in your heart. The Bible tells us that you have to ask Him in. I had no idea. So, on that day, in a hallway in front of a classroom, I asked Christ to forgive all of the bad stuff I had done and come be the Savior of my Life. And from that point, I grew in a relationship with a beautiful, kind, encouraging, faithful, fiercely loyal friend named Jesus. That was almost 20 years ago.

And yes, my life changed. So very much. There are definitely still bumps. And I still make mistakes. But I am no longer alone. And those mistakes I make are just lessons to learn from. Because they do not define me. My identity is defined by Christ and what He says about me. My identity is no longer how I feel about myself or what anyone else had to say. I learned that day that I was made in His Image. And that He shed his blood so that all of the mess from my past was dropped into the bottom of the sea. And He put a sign there that says "No Fishing."

I am a child of God. A daughter of The King, and my identity is sealed forever. And in His word, He calls me good and beautiful. He calls me blameless, beloved, blessed, righteous, chosen, complete, and a good work. He calls me a good work y'all. Twenty years later, I still fall to my knees because I know what I have done and what I have been through, and yet knowing all this He calls me His Masterpiece. And that's what he says about you. Ephesians 2:10: "For we are God's masterpiece, created in Christ Jesus to do good works, which God prepared in advance for us to do." With all of my heart, I want to be the best version of me, not because I think He will love me more, but because I love Him so much. And I am so thankful that he has plans for me. Good plans. Big plans. Things that he created just for me. And I believe Him. I have a lot of favorite verses, but my life verse is this. "Blessed is she who has believed that the Lord would fulfill His promises to her!" Luke 1:45. You guys I wake up choosing to believe Him every day. That is what faith is. Our choice to believe. To trust. And friends, the blessings have not stopped since. Some are hard blessings, like holding my mama's hand when she went home. And some are great big beautiful miraculous blessings, like my marriage to Saint Kyle. And each new day I do my best to walk in trust and I choose to believe His promises to me. And it changes everything.

At this point I could share a million God stories. Because a lot of adventures happen in twenty years, like buying a farm and writing books. But for the sake of time I will just share the latest adventure that God is taking me on.

At the end of 2017 I was having a quick lunch in the keeping room off of my kitchen. It was a beautiful fall afternoon, and all was right in my world. And while I was sitting there, God quietly and gently spoke to my heart. "You won't always be in design the way you know it." And that's all he said. I was confused. "Lord what does that mean? I don't know anything other than design. It's all I've ever done. It's all my family's ever done. What does that mean." But there was nothing more. Just crickets. And I sat there stunned, and teary-eyed. But, I said I trust you Lord. And though there was no more direct conversation about it, there seemed to be a tension lying just below the surface from then on. About eighteen months later, nearing the halfway point of 2019, the tension was mounting. And I began to pray: Lord if you are ready for me to move on just tell me what's next, and I'll go. Crickets. Each month that passed I waited for God to present me with my next career, but nothing was happening. So. I just kept taking construction and design jobs. I was also busy writing and working on So. Bell projects, but no new career was flashing its neon sign in from of me. In some ways I felt I was being disobedient—but I didn't know what I was supposed to do. My heart knew it was time to walk away from working as a design consultant, but I didn't know what I was walking in to. In October of 2019, a sweet friend who had given me wise counsel before asked me how I was doing at a conference we were preparing for. I said Tresa, God's calling me to walk away and to jump out of a plane with Him. And that's great. I'll jump with him. I'm just waiting to see what the parachute looks like. And she smiled and said like it was the most obvious thing ever…"He is the parachute." That day, I said ok Lord. I'm ready to jump. But how do I tell my husband?

It took me another couple of weeks to build up the courage to talk to Kyle. How was I going to tell him that I felt called to quit my job? And that I had no idea how I would help take care of our financial obligations, including half our living expenses and college educations? So, one morning while we were having coffee, I said, "I think God's calling me away from design as my job. Actually, I don't think, I know." He casually said, "Okay honey." I was pretty sure he was not understanding. So, I followed up with, "I think immediately. Like I won't take anymore design work. At all. I'll finish what I'm working on but by the spring of 2020, I'll be done." He then blinked for a moment. He slowly and hesitantly said, "That sounds good." And then he was quiet again. A few minutes later he said, kindly but expectantly, "How do you plan to make money?" I whispered, "I don't know. God's not told me that part yet."

It took him about a week before he mentioned it again. I did not blame him. I'd had months to process already and was still sort of shaken. I knew his hesitation wasn't because he is not a supportive husband, because he always jumps on the crazy train with me. But up until that point I had made a very substantial income. And based on numbers, If I didn't replace it, our bills wouldn't get paid. We would have to sell our home, the LTF. And kids would be taking out student loans. But I knew I had to trust God with all of that. So, when Kyle walked up to me and said, "If God is calling you to walk away, they we have to trust Him. He always provides," I knew it was going to be okay.

"Faith is climbing out on a limb, cutting it off, and watching the tree fall down."

"Faith is taking the first step before God reveals the next step."

—Mark Batterson, *Chasing the Lion*

Here's what I'm learning. Obedience is hard. But so are all good things. I still don't know what I will be doing for a living after the next few months of renovations and new constructions are complete. I have no idea how our bills will get paid or what our financial future looks like. I have no idea if anyone will buy this book, call me to speak, or watch my videos. I have no idea what my days will look like or how I will spend my time. But I have been asked to walk in Obedience and to trust that He will keep His promises. I have had a front row seat to witness His miracles. I have seen him move mountains surrounded by death and addiction. I have seen him part the waters of abuse. I have seen him bring down giants of insecurity and self-doubt. He has shut the mouths of lions and calmed the storms of disease. He has broken chains of unbelief that have ran through an entire family for far too long. And I was there when he took a broken girl and held her high in His hands and shouted Victory!

And friend, He is not finished. He will continue to shape me in all that I am designed, called, and gifted to be. Because "He who began the good work within me, will continue his work until it is finally finished on the day when Christ Jesus returns."—Philippians 1:6. And I know that I don't have to perfect. In fact, it's impossible. He knows I will make mistakes. And some will be big. But He shed His blood so that those mistakes need not keep me from where He is sending me.

I know that nothing I do can keep Him from loving me. " For I am convinced that neither death nor life, neither angels nor demons, neither the present nor the future, nor any powers, neither height nor depth, nor anything else in all creation, will be able to separate me from the love of God that is in Christ Jesus our Lord."—Romans 8:38-39.

And I know the same is true for you. He desperately loves you. And He has plans for your life that are far beyond anything you could ever imagine. If you do not know Him, just call out, because He's been waiting a long time for you. If you have known Him forever but have not invited Him into your heart, I promise that it changes everything. Invite Him. And if you have been walking with Him, for as long as you can remember, and you know of His goodness and His grace, then I beg you to reach out to a broken girl who may not. Because she is destined for more too.

Revelation 22:13

"I am the Alpha and the Omega,

the First and the Last,

the Beginning and

the End."

CONCLUSION

MY CHARGE TO YOU

I wish that when I was a little girl hiding in my closet while my parents were fighting, or a teenager crashed on a friend's couch because my family was imploding, or a young single mom exhausted and alone, that someone would have taken the time to tell me I was worthy.

So, I cannot let you close this book, and go another day without making sure you understand how very worthy you are. So, just to remind you...

You are worthy of love, kindness, and respect. That means no one has the right to hurt you. For any reason. No one has the right to put their hands on you, or to say things to break you down. No one. Ever.

Your body is worthy of honor and protection. It has been fearfully and wonderfully created and every inch of it has value. It is not to be given away or disregarded. Because you are worth more.

You are worthy of great friends who will support you and a partner who will love you like the treasure you are. And if they do not, then you have the right to walk away.

You are worthy of chasing every dream, of setting and accomplishing audacious goals, and of courageously fighting for things that bring you joy. That means you get to make the choices for your life, regardless of what anyone else says. You choose who you say you are.

And we, you and I, will not allow bullies or lies, comparison or fear, messy pasts or self-doubt, false perceptions or wrong assumptions, broken hearts or broken families, pride or prejudice, or any other giant out there to get in our way of becoming all we are designed, called, and gifted to be. Because we are fighters, you and I. We are capable. We are fierce. We are strong. And we are not afraid of giants. Because we know, regardless of what the world says, we are destined for more.

Please continue to be a part of our So. Bell & Co. community!

Stay up to date with all the happenings through our website-
www.sobellandco.com

And join us on IG and FB @sobellandco

We also love old school correspondence as well. Our snail mail address is
PO BOX 81146, Midland, TX 79708

ACKNOWLEDGEMENTS

Thank you to my boys. You make me better in the most wonderful ways. My greatest achievement is being your mom.

Thank you to my joy crew, you know who you are, thank you for believing that my words may help others. Joy comes next!

To my friends who let me crash your homes to write, this book is here because of your generosity, I love you more than pumpkin cheesecake and donkeys.

To my ex-husband. Thank you for letting me share part of our past, to give others hope.

Thank you to my editor Tori, God created you to capture thoughts. Hold words. Create beauty. And help each one of us release a magnum opus. I feel so blessed that my project was in your hands. We will forever be bonded through the pursuit of "Golf and Life."

To Patrick Payton, my brother from another mother. Thank you for fighting with me, and encouraging me to become all I am "Designed, Called, and Gifted" to be. The principle that not only changed my life but became my "why." You better get that book going ASAP. I'm ready to teach.

And last but certainly not least…

To "Carl". "Cow Bird." "Special K." "Deuce." "Saint Kyle." Thank you for always jumpin' on the crazy train without asking where we are going. You are my best friend and my anchor. My person. My pal. My partner. I love you more than words. Consider this the first of many "literary thank yous."

ABOUT THE AUTHOR

With more than two decades in the design industry and a love for "All Things Home," Brandy Bell decided to bring her heart for teaching and encouraging women to the forefront of her business endeavors. In 2012, she founded Southern Bell and Company—or So. Bell & Co. as her community has come to know it—a multimedia Lifestyle and Design start up that includes blogging, videos, live workshoppes, women's conferences, and an annual Marketplace that benefits local female entrepreneurs and a variety of family based charities in the West Texas area.

Along with public speaking and writing, Brandy enjoys any opportunity to encourage women to fearlessly pursue their dreams. She and her husband, Kyle, live with a multiplicity of codependent animals on their "Little Teeny Farm" in Midland, Texas.